The Greater Manchester Boundary Walk

Graham Phythian

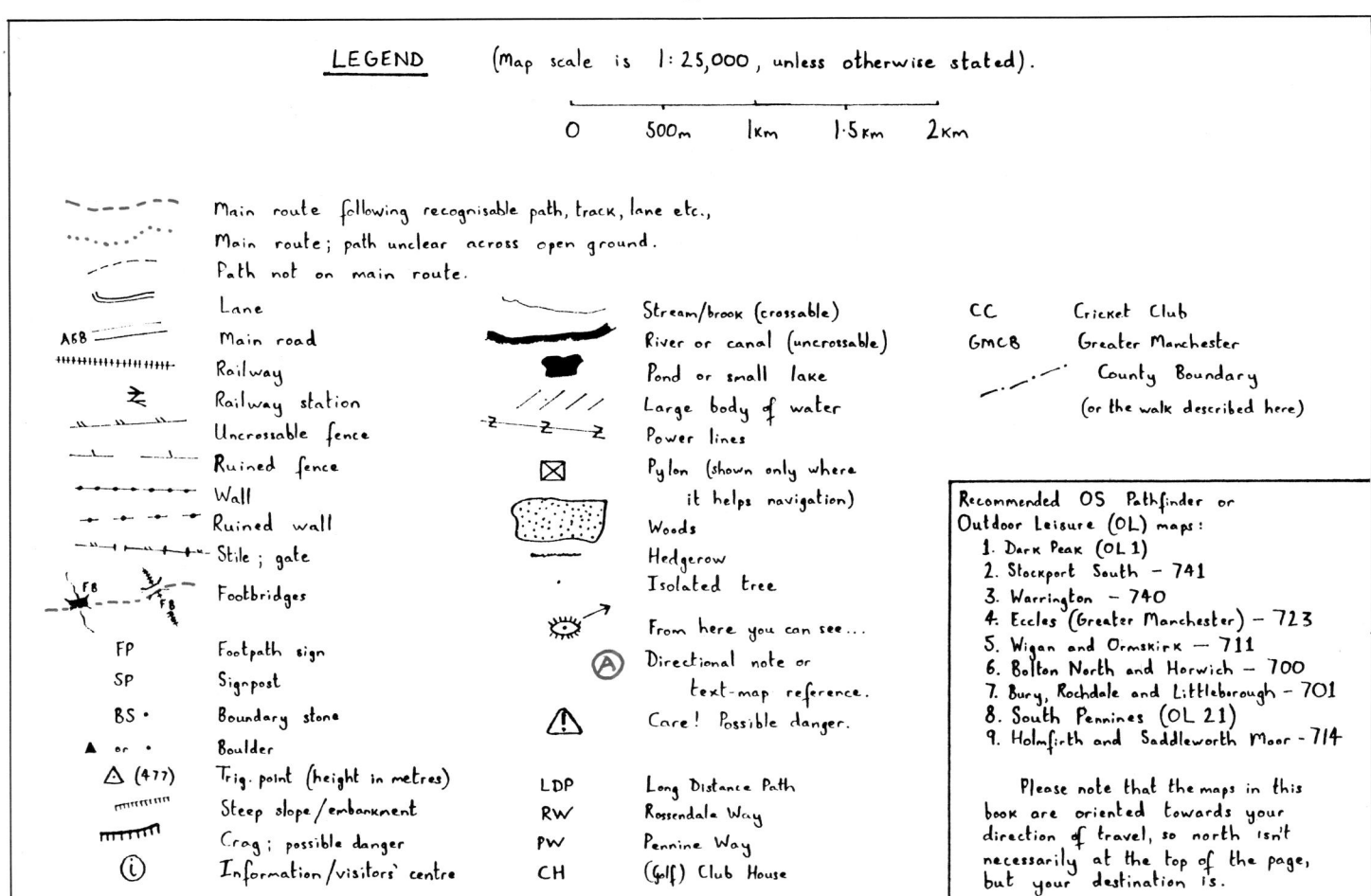

LEGEND (map scale is 1:25,000, unless otherwise stated).

0   500m   1km   1·5km   2km

Main route following recognisable path, track, lane etc.,

Main route; path unclear across open ground.

Path not on main route.

Lane

A68 Main road

Railway

Railway station

Uncrossable fence

Ruined fence

Wall

Ruined wall

Stile ; gate

FB Footbridges

FP Footpath sign

SP Signpost

BS · Boundary stone

▲ or • Boulder

△ (477) Trig. point (height in metres)

Steep slope/embankment

Crag ; possible danger

ⓘ Information/visitors' centre

Stream/brook (crossable)

River or canal (uncrossable)

Pond or small lake

Large body of water

Power lines

⊠ Pylon (shown only where
it helps navigation)

Woods

Hedgerow

· Isolated tree

From here you can see...

Ⓐ Directional note or
text-map reference.

⚠ Care! Possible danger.

LDP Long Distance Path

RW Rossendale Way

PW Pennine Way

CH (Golf) Club House

CC Cricket Club

GMCB Greater Manchester

County Boundary

(or the walk described here)

Recommended OS Pathfinder or
Outdoor Leisure (OL) maps:
1. Dark Peak (OL 1)
2. Stockport South — 741
3. Warrington — 740
4. Eccles (Greater Manchester) — 723
5. Wigan and Ormskirk — 711
6. Bolton North and Horwich — 700
7. Bury, Rochdale and Littleborough — 701
8. South Pennines (OL 21)
9. Holmfirth and Saddleworth Moor — 714

   Please note that the maps in this
book are oriented towards your
direction of travel, so north isn't
necessarily at the top of the page,
but your destination is.

THE GREATER MANCHESTER COUNTY
– a boundary walk.

Contents

INTRODUCTION

Why Greater Manchester?

More people live within a 60km radius of Tintwistle than within a similar radius of the centre of London. (For those of us who know Tintwistle, a tiny dry-stone hamlet clinging to the main A628 Longdendale Road, 3km north of Glossop, this may come as something of a surprise.)

This means that upwards of 7,000,000 people have fairly easy access to:

Etherow / Goyt Valley
Derbyshire Peak District
Cheshire Green Belt
Bollin Valley
Douglas Valley
Lancashire Moors
Pennine Way and Southerly Yorkshire Dales

Now it's a happy coincidence that the outer boundary of the ten boroughs that make up the Greater Manchester conurbation: Tameside, Stockport, City of Manchester, Trafford, Salford, Wigan, Bolton, Bury, Rochdale and Oldham, passes through or near several areas of natural beauty, several areas which have been landscaped and successfully reclaimed from the decay of old industries, and yet more that seem to breathe history from the very earth and stones. (The pace is slower on the periphery; imagination has more time to work it's spell on you.)

So, most people in this region of the North of England can get to some of the best walking country around, at the outside two hours away on public transport.

The grand tour proposed here is designed to satisfy most walkers' needs:

- The country lane stroller, out for an afternoon or evening to observe nature and perhaps work up a thirst;
- The one who responds to a challenge, and wants to do the lot in four days or less (not recommended, as you'll miss a lot!);
- The omnivorously interested type: flora, fauna, real ale, geography, geology, history, real ale, farming, canals, architecture and real ale — everything is grist to this person's mill. They could take a year or so to complete the walk, an odd day or weekend at a time;
- Lastly, the one that inspired the idea in the first place: the townie (like myself) who has been toying with the idea of tackling a long-distance path, but hasn't got the time or the confidence to go for the Pennine Way or the Offa's Dyke just yet.

So as you can see, you can indulge in one long gourmet feast of walking, or attack the round in bite-sized chunks. Nearly all the sections start and finish near a railway station or on a bus route. Accommodation is almost invariably easy to find, within a few kilometres of the recommended route.

Why Woolley Bridge ?

You don't have to start here, of course.

Stand on the bridge over the River Etherow, though, and you are bang on the GMCB; you have a choice of nice pubs for the sneck-lifter before the journey (and, perhaps more importantly, at the end of it, too!); and you have the signs for GLOSSOP - DERBYSHIRE and TAMESIDE - HOLLINGWORTH on opposite sides of the road as visual evidence of the boundary you are about to walk.

But the best reasons for Woolley Bridge are linked to the reasons:

Why Clockwise ?

A touch of stage-management, really.

If you go clockwise from Woolley Bridge:

- The Derbyshire and Cheshire Hills you encounter almost immediately whet your appetite for the Moors of the second half of the walk;

- You have the prevailing westerly weather against you during the lowland stretch, where its effect is negligible;

- during the dull bits you have Winter Hill beckoning on the skyline to keep you going;

- best of all the hill and moorland scenery just gets better and better, with the dramatic climax of Chew Valley on the last day.

Why this precise route?

No particular reason.

You may discover better, more attractive pathways. You may be tempted to leave the route altogether and explore the country further out from the GMCB. You may want to visit a maiden aunt in Chorley or Buxton who does a nice line in fruit cake and high teas etc, etc,

In devising the route given here, I set myself a condition: to keep within about 2km of the GMCB all the way round. Following the boundary exactly is only for those training for the SAS or for young males wishing to deliver chocolates to their lady friends in the dead of night, as you'll have to sprint across the tarmac on the main runway at Manchester International Airport, hang-glide across the quarry on Scout Moor near Ramsbottom, dodge across seven motorways, and swim 3km down the middle of the Manchester Ship Canal. I didn't want the book to have to carry a Government Health warning, so within 2km or so it had to be. The only time I bent the rule was for an excellent reason - as you'll see towards the end of the trek.

Why don't you just get out there and do it?

How to get to Woolley Bridge:
Bus or train from Central Manchester. Destination: Glossop. Nearest railway station is Dinting (railway museum, walk along Glossop Brook). 2km away from the "start".

Take:
Spare clothing - it can get cold suddenly on the tops!
Spare T-shirt in hot weather. You don't want your sweat cooling on your back;

Maps;
Compass - always useful, even if it looks easy;
Insect repellent, and some salve for abrasions
Waterproofs;
This book!

Are you a daily dabbler or an all-at-once obsessive? If the latter, check out accommodation beforehand. In any case, check out bus and train availability and schedules.

For footgear, trainers are OK in the lowlands, so long as it's fairly dry. Best of all, though, is a good pair of walking boots. Make sure you break them in first!

Timing: allow about 3km per hour. This seems very slow, but is intended to include time for stops, rough or steep terrain and conversations and other distractions en route.

THE COUNTRY CODE

1. Respect those who live and work in the country
2. Don't make a nuisance of yourself with litter or unnecessary noise.
3. Use public paths, gates and stiles
4. Don't pollute the water
5. Don't interfere with crops or livestock
6. Fasten gates after you.
7. Guard against risk of fire
8. Protect all wildlife, trees and plants
9. If you must take your dog - keep it under control.

The information leaflet on the Healey Dell Nature Trail puts the spirit of the code beautifully:

" DON'T LEAVE ANYTHING BUT FOOTPRINTS

DON'T TAKE ANYTHING BUT PHOTOGRAPHS

DON'T KILL ANYTHING BUT TIME "

Mellor Church (viewed from the south west)   R.F.
See map on page 10

| WOOLLEY BRIDGE to MOORFIELD ARMS (8 km) | START at the BOTTOM of the PAGE, and work your way up. All the map texts are to be read like this. | ↓ N |

At this early stage, you may be tempted already to abandon (or postpone) the GMCB, as the Derbyshire hills present an alluring vista to your left and ahead, as they dissolve, fold upon fold, into the misty distance. If you do stray, the Dark Peak Outdoor Leisure Map will show you dozens of pathways over to Edale, Castleton and Chapel.

Kinder Downfall

PH Moorfield Arms (Robinson's) Good pub grub served 12 - 2 pm. Banks' Ale.

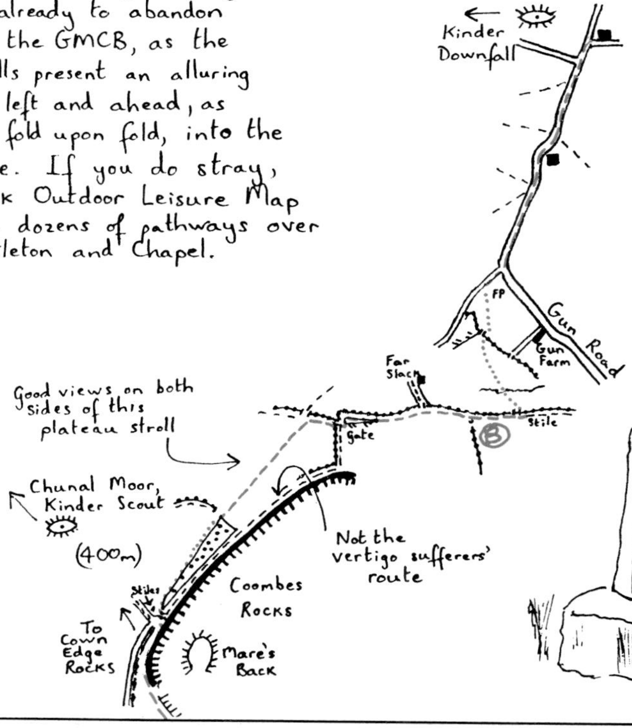

FP

Gun Road

Gun Farm

Far Slack

Good views on both sides of this plateau stroll

Gate

Stile

Ⓑ

Ⓑ Robin Hood's Picking Rods. These are thought to be old boundary stones. The legend that links them to the outlaw goes as follows: an evil baron would only agree to a young girl in his charge to be released for marriage to her lover, if Robin could hit the stones from a great distance with one out of three arrows. He succeeded with the third. You can still see the mark where the arrow is said to have struck.

Chunal Moor, Kinder Scout

(400 m)

Not the vertigo sufferers' route

Stile

Coombes Rocks

To Cown Edge Rocks

Mare's Back

All of Glossop and its surrounding forest and moorland was given by Henry III. in the ⑬ to the Cistercian Monks of Basingwerke Abbey (N. Wales). The densely forested lowlands weren't of much use, but the Monks used the moorland tops for sheep-rearing. The first "road" across the rough terrain was a raised causeway, which followed the route of the present Monks Road.

A wheatear's distinctive tail.

Wheatears make their nests in the dry-stone walls. The black and white tails are a give-away. Summer colours are grey on top, and buff below.

MELANDRA ROMAN FORT. A.D. 85-ish

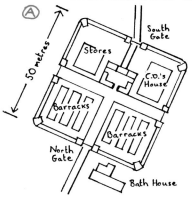

Ⓐ ← 50 metres →

- Stores
- C.O.'s House
- Barracks
- Barracks
- South Gate
- North Gate
- Bath House

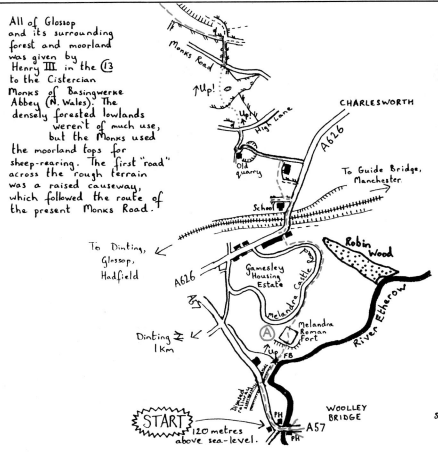

Monks Road
↑Up!
↑Up!
High Lane
Old quarry
CHARLESWORTH
A626
To Guide Bridge, Manchester.
School
Robin Wood
To Dinting, Glossop, Hadfield
A626
A57
Gamesley Housing Estate
Melandra Castle Road
River Etherow
Dinting 1 Km
Ⓐ
Melandra Roman Fort
↑Up FB
Disused railway embankment
START
120 metres above sea-level.
PH
A57
PH
WOOLLEY BRIDGE

Don't expect anything too spectacular at Melandra. All that remains is an enclosure of earthbanks, most of the stones having been taken to help build Mottram Church and parts of Woolley Bridge itself.

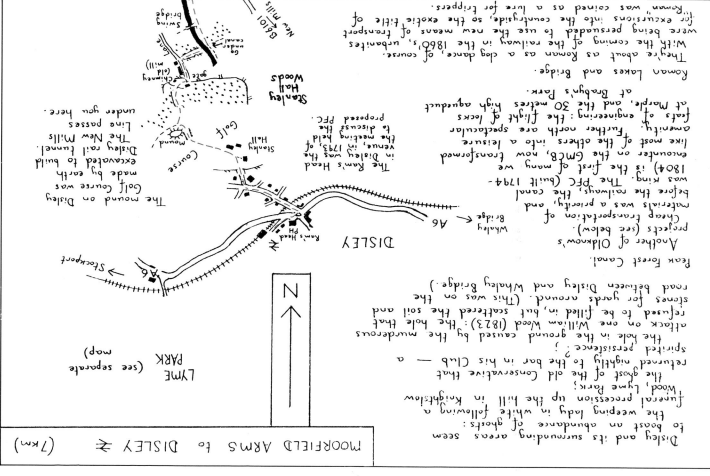

MOORFIELD ARMS to DISLEY (≈ 7km)

N

LYME PARK (see separate map)

Disley and its surrounding areas seem to boast an abundance of ghosts: the weeping lady in white following a funeral procession up the hill in Knightslow Wood, Lyme Park; the ghost of the old Conservative that returned nightly to the bar in his Club — a spirited persistence; the hole in the ground caused by the murderous attack on one William Wood (1823): the hole that refused to be filled in, but scattered the soil and stones for yards around. (This was on the road between Disley and Whaley Bridge.)

Peak Forest Canal.

Another of Oldknow's projects (see below). Cheap transportation of materials was a priority, and before the railways, the canal was king. The PFC (built 1794-1804) is the first of many we encounter on the GMCB, now transformed like most of the others into a leisure amenity. Further north are spectacular feats of engineering: the flight of locks at Marple, and the 30 metres high aqueduct at Brabyn's Park.

Roman Lakes and Bridge

They're about as Roman as a dog dance, of course. With the coming of the railway in the 1860's, urbanites were being persuaded to use the new means of transport for excursions into the countryside, so the exotic title of Roman was coined as a lure for trippers.

The mound on Disley Golf Course was made by earth excavated to build Disley rail tunnel, The New Mills Line passes under you here.

The Ram's Head in Disley was the venue, in 1793, of the meeting held to discuss the proposed PFC.

DISLEY
← Stockport A6
A6 → Whaley Bridge
Ram's Head Ph

Stanley Hall Woods
Stanley Hall
Golf Course
mound
Golf

Chimney (old mill)
go under canal
aqueduct
Swing bridge
New mills B6101

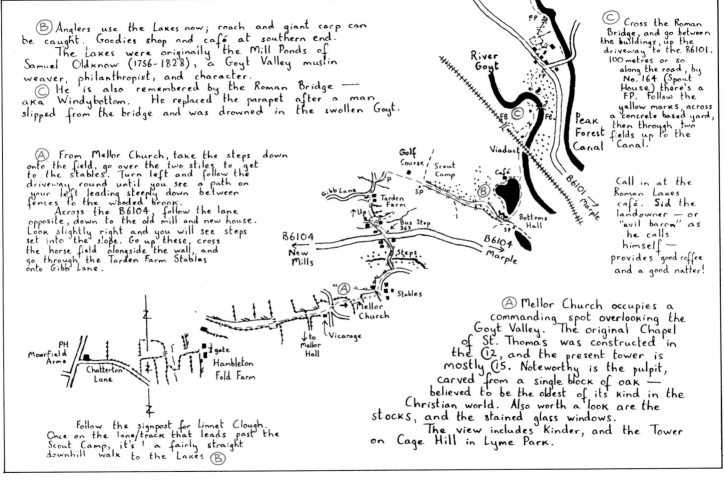

(B) Anglers use the Lakes now; roach and giant carp can be caught. Goodies shop and café at southern end.

The Lakes were originally the Mill Ponds of Samuel Oldknow (1756-1828), a Goyt Valley muslin weaver, philanthropist, and character.

(C) He is also remembered by the Roman Bridge — aka Windybottom. He replaced the parapet after a man slipped from the bridge and was drowned in the swollen Goyt.

(A) From Mellor Church, take the steps down onto the field, go over the two stiles to get to the stables. Turn left and follow the driveway round until you see a path on your left leading steeply down between fences to the wooded brook.

Across the B6104, follow the lane opposite, down to the old mill and new house. Look slightly right and you will see steps set into the slope. Go up these, cross the horse field alongside the wall, and go through the Tarden Farm Stables onto Gibb Lane.

(C) Cross the Roman Bridge, and go between the buildings, up the driveway to the B6101. 100 metres or so along the road, by No. 164 (Spout House) there's a FP. Follow the yellow marks, across a concrete based yard, then through two fields up to the Canal.

Call in at the Roman Lakes café. Sid the landowner — or "avil baron" as he calls himself — provides good coffee and a good natter!

Follow the signpost for Linnet Clough. Once on the lane/track that leads past the Scout Camp, it's a fairly straight downhill walk to the Lakes (B)

(A) Mellor Church occupies a commanding spot overlooking the Goyt Valley. The original Chapel of St. Thomas was constructed in the (12, and the present tower is mostly (15. Noteworthy is the pulpit, carved from a single block of oak — believed to be the oldest of its kind in the Christian world. Also worth a look are the stocks, and the stained glass windows.

The view includes Kinder, and the Tower on Cage Hill in Lyme Park.

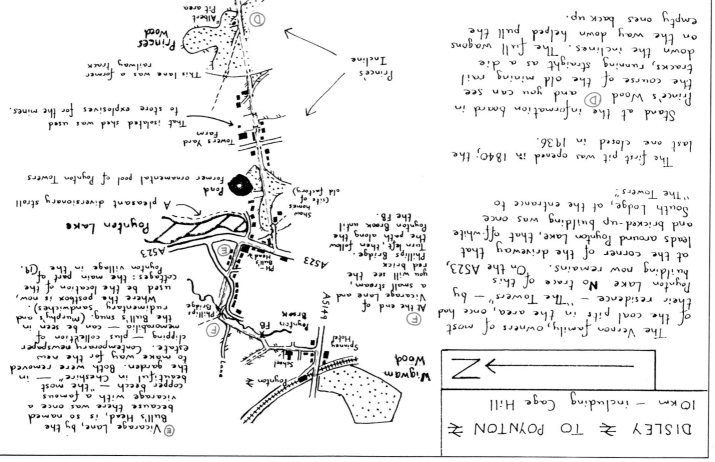

DISLEY to POYNTON
10 km – including Cage Hill

N →

The Vernon family, owners of most of the coal pits in the area, once had their residence – "The Towers" – by Poynton Lake. No trace of this building now remains. On the A523, at the corner of the driveway that leads around Poynton Lake, that off-white and bricked-up building was once South Lodge, of the entrance to "The Towers".

The first pit was opened in 1840, the last one closed in 1936.

(D) Stand at the information board in Prince's Wood and you can see the course of the old mining rail tracks, running straight as a die down the inclines. The full wagons on the way down helped pull the empty ones back up.

Albert Pit area

Princes Wood

This lane was a former railway track

Prince's Incline

That isolated shed was used to store explosives for the mines.

Towers Yard Farm

Pond — former ornamental pool of Poynton Towers

A pleasant diversionary stroll

Poynton Lake

A523

Show homes (site of old factory)

Turn left, then follow the path along the Poynton Brook until the FB.

Phillips Bridge

Poynton Brook

(F) At the end of Vicarage Lane and a small stream, you will see the red brick

A5149

Spinney Hotel

School

Poynton

Wigwam Wood

Bull's Head

(E) Vicarage Lane, by the Bull's Head, is so named because there was once a vicarage with a famous copper beech — "the most beautiful in Cheshire" — in the garden. Both were removed to make way for the new estate. Contemporary newspaper clipping — plus collection of memorabilia — can be seen in the Bull's snug (Murphy's and rudimentary sandwiches). Where the postbox is now, used be the location of the cottages: the main part of Poynton village in 1841.

The adjustable bridge over the canal has had extra layers of stone added to its structure, to allow for subsidence.

The detour by Redlegs Ⓒ is to see what's left of Vernon Wharf, where barges were once laden with coal, to sample the Middlewood Way, and to partake of refreshment at the Boar's Head. Not forgetting the delicious ice-cream sold at the shop next door.

If in a hurry, just go over the stile and follow the path by Redlegs.

There are conflicting stories as to the original purpose of the Cage. Ⓐ A prison? A vantage point for observing the hunt?

In any case, on a clear day and with a pair of binoculars, you can see across and around the vast urban bowl. The view to the south and east is dominated by the Park.

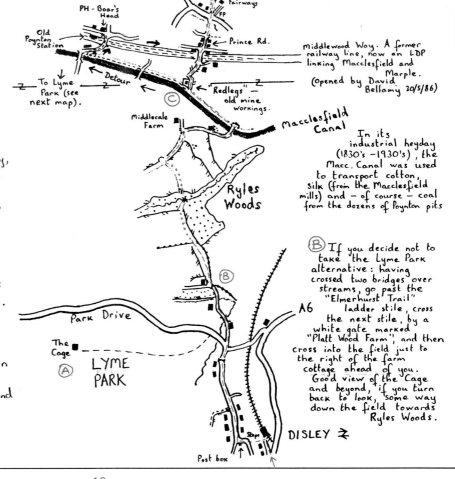

Middlewood Way. A former railway line, now an LDP linking Macclesfield and Marple. (Opened by David Bellamy 30/5/86)

In its industrial heyday (1830's -1930's), the Macc. Canal was used to transport cotton, silk (from the Macclesfield mills) and — of course — coal from the dozens of Poynton pits

Ⓑ If you decide not to take the Lyme Park alternative: having crossed two bridges over streams, go past the "Elmerhurst Trail" ladder stile, cross the next stile, by a white gate marked "Platt Wood Farm", and then cross into the field just to the right of the farm cottage ahead of you. Good view of the Cage and beyond, if you turn back to look, some way down the field towards Ryles Woods.

LYME PARK to MACCLESFIELD CANAL

Alternative route to take in deer park, Lyme Hall and gardens.

Add a kilometre or two if you go this way, depending on how much walking you decide to do in the Park.

Scale of this map: 1:10,000

500 metres

You can see the dark wooded bluff of Alderley Edge away to the south-west. Most of the left-hand view is taken up by the great west Cheshire plain, across which the river Bollin — "the ever-rolling Bollin" — snakes its green way.

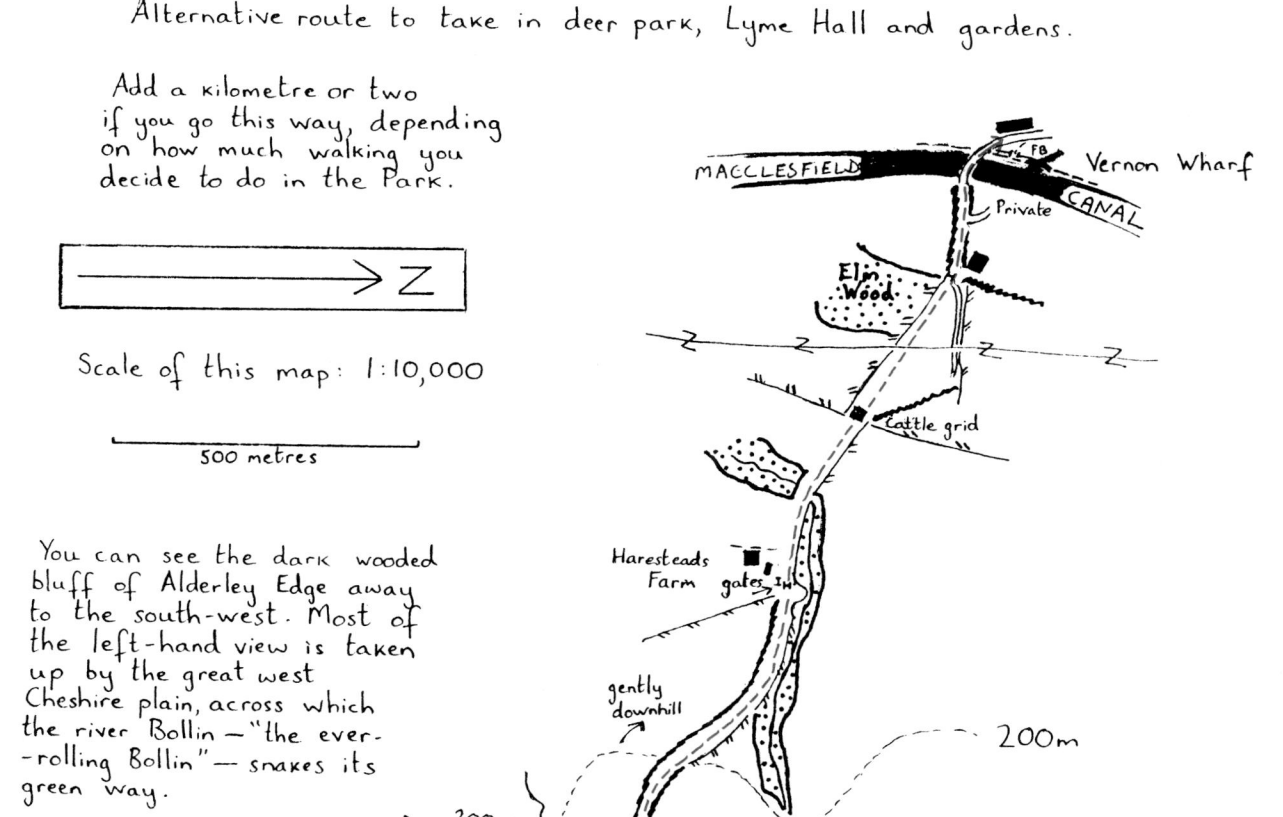

MACCLESFIELD   FB   Vernon Wharf   CANAL

Private

Elm Wood

Cattle grid

Haresteads Farm   gates

gently downhill

200m

200m

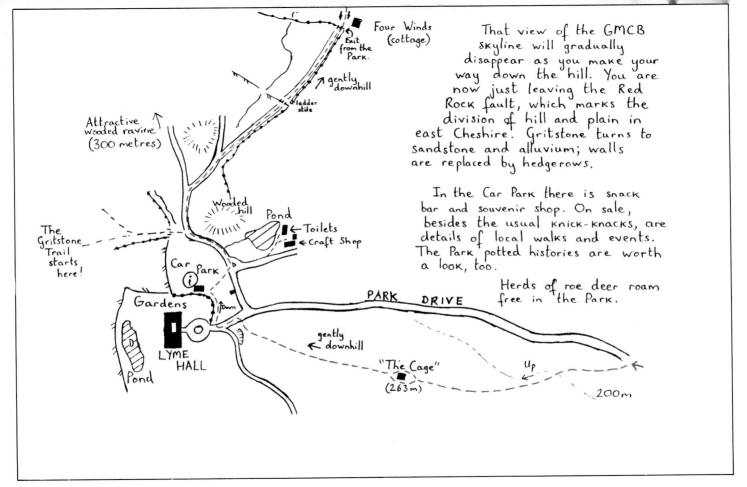

That view of the GMCB skyline will gradually disappear as you make your way down the hill. You are now just leaving the Red Rock fault, which marks the division of hill and plain in east Cheshire. Gritstone turns to sandstone and alluvium; walls are replaced by hedgerows.

In the Car Park there is snack bar and souvenir shop. On sale, besides the usual knick-knacks, are details of local walks and events. The Park potted histories are worth a look, too.

Herds of roe deer roam free in the Park.

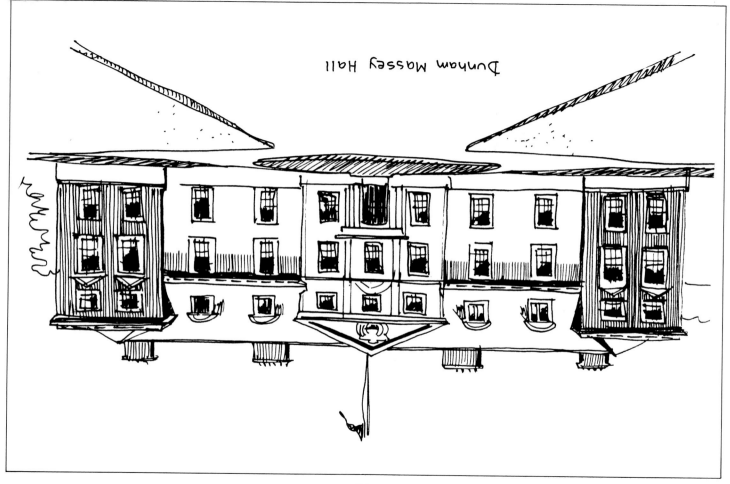

Dunham Massey Hall

St. Bartholomew's Church, Wilmslow   R.F.

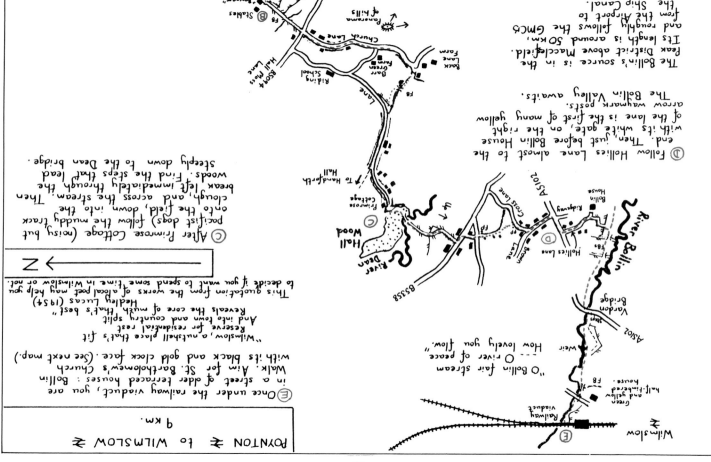

↑ N

Ⓔ Once under the railway viaduct, you are in a street of older terraced houses : Bollin Walk. Aim for St. Bartholomew's Church with its black and gold clock face. (See next map.)

"Wilmslow, a nutshell place that's fit
Reserve for residential rest
And into town and country split
Reveals the core of much that's best."
Hedley Lucas (1954)

This quotation from the works of a local poet may help you to decide if you want to spend some time in Wilmslow or not.

Ⓒ After Primrose Cottage (noisy but pacifist dogs) follow the muddy track onto the field, and down into the clough, and across the stream. Then break left immediately through the woods. Find the steps that lead steeply down to the Dean bridge.

The Bollin's source is in the Peak District above Macclesfield. Its length is around 50 km, and roughly follows the GMC5 from the Airport to the Ship Canal.

The Bollin Valley awaits.

arrow waymark posts.
of the lane is the first of many yellow
with its white gate, on the right
end. Then, just before Bollin House
Ⓓ Follow Hollies Lane almost to the

"O Bollin fair stream
O river of peace
How lovely you flow."

Wilmslow

Map labels:
"Bowness", FB, Stables Ⓑ, Panorama of hills, Church Lane, Hall Moss Lane, B5094, Riding School, Barn Lane Farm, Back Lane, FB, Lane, Hall, To Handforth, Primrose Cottage Ⓒ, Hall Wood, River Dean, Cross Lane, A5102, Ridgeway, Bollin House, Hollies Lane Ⓓ, FBs, Brook Lane, B5358, River Bollin, Vardon Bridge, A5102, Weir, FB, Green and yellow half-timbered house, Railway viaduct Ⓔ

This is the first and only significant brush with suburbia on the GMCB. To compensate, there are attractive lanes and cottages en route, but most of this section can be tackled at a fairly smart pace. At least, until the River Dean.

How to date a hedgerow: in a length of 25 metres, 1 species of shrub = 100 years (appx.).

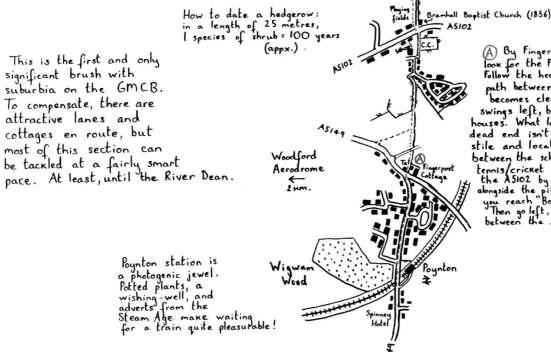

Ⓐ By Fingerpost Cottage: look for the FP and stile. Follow the hedgerow until a path between fences becomes clear, and then swings left, behind the houses. What looks like a dead end isn't. Climb the stile and locate the path between the school and the tennis/cricket terrain. Cross the A5102 by the church, go alongside the "pitches until you reach "Bowness". Ⓑ Then go left, on the path between the fences.

Poynton station is a photogenic jewel. Potted plants, a wishing-well, and adverts from the Steam Age make waiting for a train quite pleasurable!

Playing fields
Bramhall Baptist Church (1856)
A5102
A5102
School
C.C.
A5149
Woodford Aerodrome
← 2 km.
Tel.
Ⓐ Fingerpost Cottage
Wigwam Wood
Poynton
Spinney Hotel
A5149

WILMSLOW ⇄ to CASTLE MILL (8km)

Trees along the Bollin:

Oak
Beech
Silver Birch
Fir
S O L
Willow
Poplar
Larch
Beech

(See inset map overleaf.)

Ⓐ **Crossing the A538:**
The footpath sneaks along the left bank of the Bollin, between the lane and the busy A538. Once across the main road, go down some steps and cross a stile with a yellow arrow. Aim for a wooded slope ahead of you, crossing a wooden footbridge en route.

Manchester International Airport: 10 million passengers each year (1990). A new terminal proposed; estimated 23 million passengers annually by the end of the century.

N ←

Some OS maps are wrong hereabouts, because of recent developments.

This is a good spot to examine aeroplanes' undercarriages. Take some cotton wool, though.

Follow the SP – "Pigley Stairs".

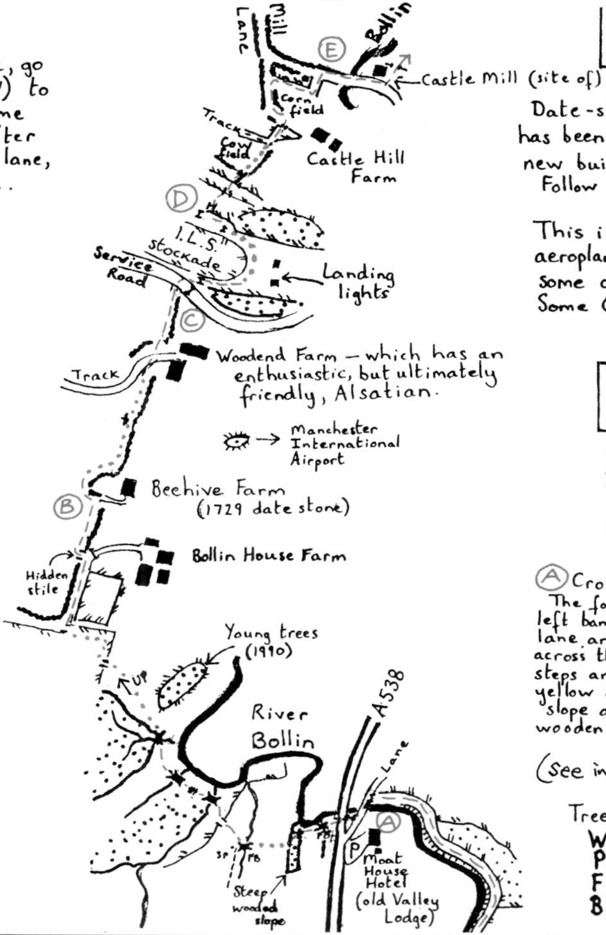

Date-stone from the original Mill has been preserved as part of the new building.

Castle Mill (site of)

All of this section is very well signposted, either with the yellow arrow symbol, or with the smart "Bollin Valley Project" symbols. Information boards seem almost as plentiful as the grey squirrels.

Ⓑ Cross the stile into Beehive Farm Drive. Turn left to reach the end of the tall hedge (10 metres). The stile into the next field is here.

(* ILS = Instrument Landing System.)

Ⓒ Ignore that nice Service Road with the cattle grid, and make your way round, keeping to the wooden stockade fence, all the way round, and cross the stile in the "bottleneck" corner.

After Beehive Farm: Follow the redundant stiles, until you reach the ILS* stockade.

Ⓓ **From ILS fence to Mill Lane:**
Turn away from the stockade, go over a series of stiles (roughly NW) to go along the edge of a cow field. Some farm houses appear on the right. After a triangular field, go left along the lane, then along the far edge of a corn field. When you see a post with an arrow on it, cut left along a track, until you emerge on Mill Lane.

Ⓔ you emerge on Mill Lane.

Map labels:

Moat House Hotel (old Valley Lodge)
Steep Wooded slope
Moat Lane
A538
River Bollin
Rut
Young trees (1910)
Bollin House Farm
Hidden stile
Beehive Farm (1729 date stone)
← Manchester International Airport
Wooded Farm – which has an enthusiastic, but ultimately friendly, Alsatian.
Landing lights
Track
Service Road
Stockade
I.L.S.
Castle Hill Farm
Track
Castle Mill (site of)
Mill Lane
Corn field
field

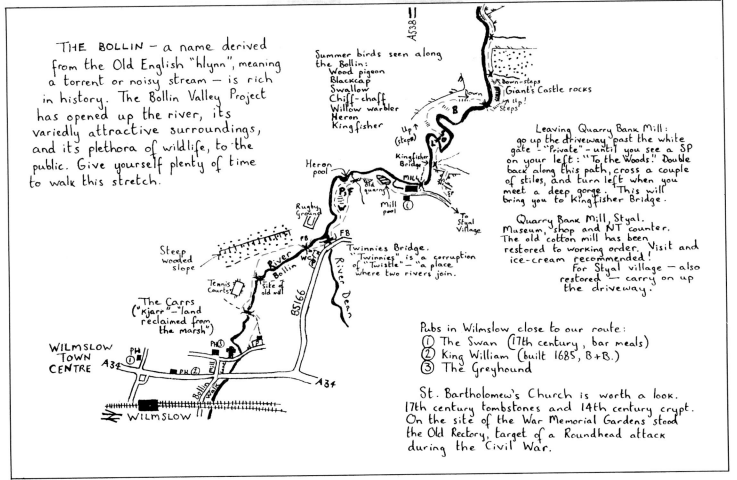

THE BOLLIN — a name derived from the Old English "hlynn", meaning a torrent or noisy stream — is rich in history. The Bollin Valley Project has opened up the river, its variedly attractive surroundings, and it's plethora of wildlife, to the public. Give yourself plenty of time to walk this stretch.

Summer birds seen along the Bollin:
Wood pigeon
Blackcap
Swallow
Chiff-chaff
Willow warbler
Heron
Kingfisher

Leaving Quarry Bank Mill: go up the driveway past the white gate – "Private" – until you see a SP on your left: "To the Woods!" Double back along this path, cross a couple of stiles, and turn left when you meet a deep gorge. This will bring you to Kingfisher Bridge.

Quarry Bank Mill, Styal. Museum, shop and NT counter. The old cotton mill has been restored to working order. Visit and ice-cream recommended! For Styal village — also restored — carry on up the driveway.

Twinnies Bridge. "Twinnies" is a corruption of "Twistle" — "a place where two rivers join."

The Carrs ("Kjarr" – "land reclaimed from the marsh")

WILMSLOW TOWN CENTRE

Pubs in Wilmslow close to our route:
① The Swan (17th century, bar meals)
② King William (built 1685, B+B.)
③ The Greyhound

St. Bartholomew's Church is worth a look. 17th century tombstones and 14th century crypt. On the site of the War Memorial Gardens stood the Old Rectory, target of a Roundhead attack during the Civil War.

Quarry Bank Mill, Styal

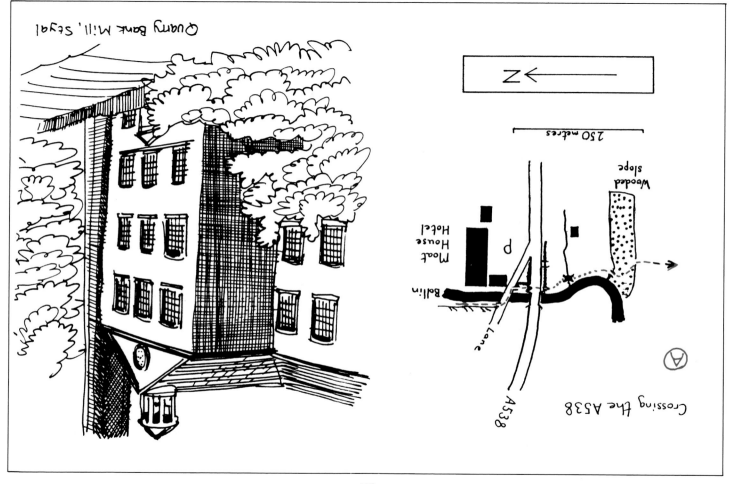

← N

250 metres

Wooded slope

Moat House Hotel

Ballin Lane

A538

Crossing the A538

Dunham Massey Mill

RF

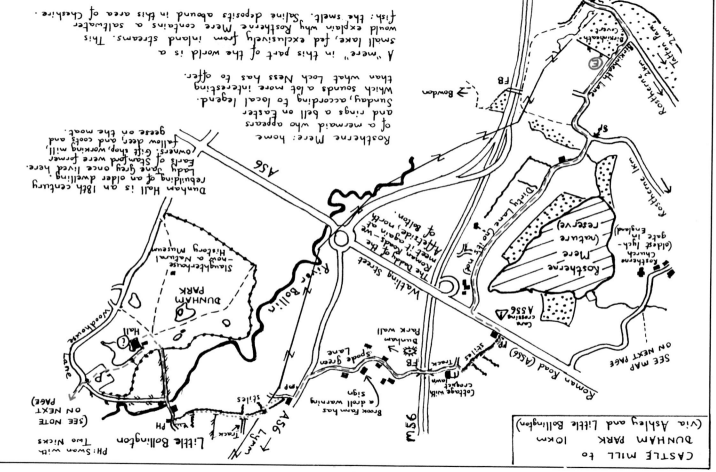

A "mere" in this part of the world is a small lake, fed exclusively from inland streams. This would explain why Rostherne Mere contains a saltwater fish: the smelt. Saline deposits abound in this area of Cheshire.

Rostherne Mere: home of a mermaid who appears and rings a bell on Easter Sunday, according to local legend. Which sounds a lot more interesting than what Loch Ness has to offer.

Dunham Hall is an 18th century rebuilding of an older dwelling. Lady Jane Grey once lived here. Earls of Stamford were former owners. Gift shop, working mill, fallow deer, and coots and geese on the moat.

The Road of the Roman Roads — we meet it again at Alfeside, north of Bolton.

Bowdon →

← 2

F8

3

Rostherne Lane

Birkinheath Court

Tatton Park 2km

st

Rostherne Inn

Dirty Lane Crofts

Rostherne Mere (nature reserve)

Rostherne Church (oldest lych-gate in England)

Cars crossing A556

SEE MAP ON NEXT PAGE

Roman Road (A556)

A56

River Bollin

DUNHAM PARK

Woodhouse Lane

Hall

P

Slaughterhouse — now a Natural History Museum

Watling Street

Alfeside to Bolton

Dunham Park wall

Spode Green Lane

stiles

FB

Cottage with croquet lawn

Track

stiles

FB

Brook Farm has a droll warning sign

stiles

Track

rap

A56

Lymm →

Little Bollington

PH

Track

(SEE NOTE ON NEXT PAGE)

PH: Swan with Two Nicks

P

M56

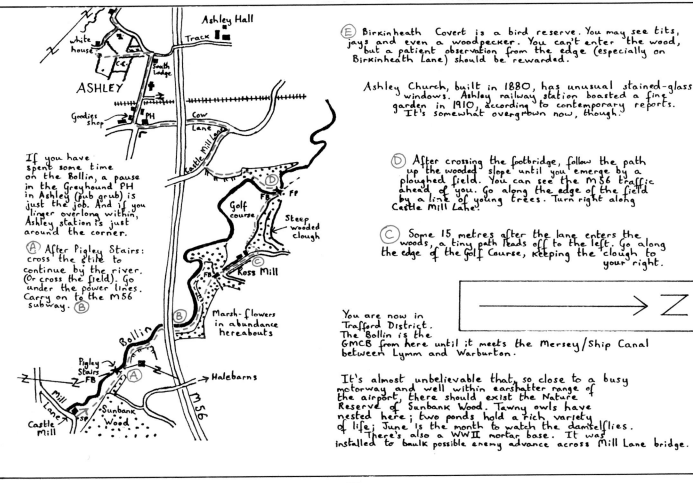

E Birkinheath Covert is a bird reserve. You may see tits, jays and even a woodpecker. You can't enter the wood, but a patient observation from the edge (especially on Birkinheath Lane) should be rewarded.

Ashley Church, built in 1880, has unusual stained-glass windows. Ashley railway station boasted a fine garden in 1910, according to contemporary reports. It's somewhat overgrown now, though.

D After crossing the footbridge, follow the path up the wooded slope until you emerge by a ploughed field. You can see the M56 traffic ahead of you. Go along the edge of the field by a line of young trees. Turn right along Castle Mill Lane.

C Some 15 metres after the lane enters the woods, a tiny path leads off to the left. Go along the edge of the Golf Course, keeping the clough to your right.

You are now in Trafford District. The Bollin is the GMCB from here until it meets the Mersey/Ship Canal between Lymm and Warburton.

It's almost unbelievable that, so close to a busy motorway and well within earshatter range of the airport, there should exist the Nature Reserve of Sunbank Wood. Tawny owls have nested here; two ponds hold a rich variety of life; June is the month to watch the damselflies.
There's also a WWII mortar base. It was installed to baulk possible enemy advance across Mill Lane bridge.

If you have spent some time on the Bollin, a pause in the Greyhound PH in Ashley (pub grub) is just the job. And if you linger overlong within, Ashley station is just around the corner.

A After Pigley Stairs: cross the stile to continue by the river. (Or cross the field). Go under the power lines. Carry on to the M56 subway. **B**

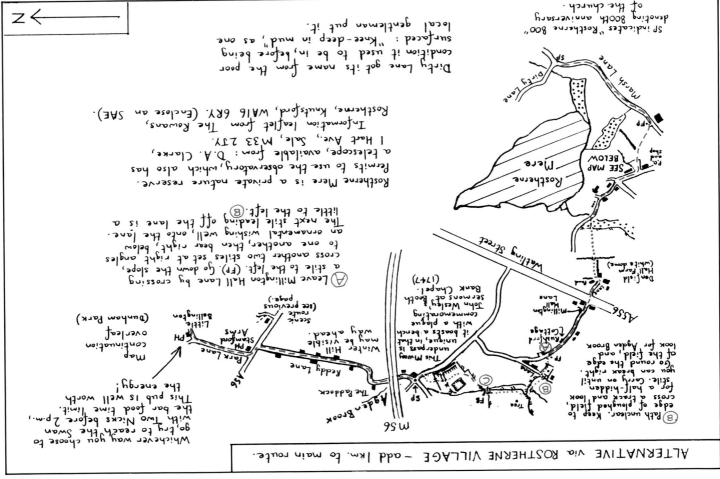

ALTERNATIVE via ROSTHERNE VILLAGE – add 1km. to main route.

N

SP indicates "Rostherne 800", denoting 800th anniversary of the church.

Dirty Lane got its name from the poor condition it used to be in, before being surfaced: "Knee-deep in mud", as one local gentleman put it.

Rostherne Mere is a private nature reserve. Permits to use the observatory, which also has a telescope available from: D.A. Clarke, 1 Hart Ave., Sale, M33 2TY.
Information leaflet from The Rowans, Rostherne, Knutsford, WA16 6RY. (Enclose an SAE).

The next stile leading off the lane is a little to the left (B).

Ⓐ Leave Millington Hall Lane by crossing a stile to the left (FP). Go down the slope, cross another two stiles set at right angles to one another, then bear right, below an ornamental wishing well, onto the lane.

Dirty Lane
Marsh Lane
sp
FP
PO. and shop
SEE MAP BELOW
Rostherne Mere
Denfield Hall Farm (white dome)
Watling Street
A556
Millington Lane
Rushford Cottage
FP
look for Agden Brook.

Ⓑ Path unclear. Keep to edge of ploughed field, cross a track and look for a half-hidden stile. Carry on until you can break right, go round the edge of the field, and look for Agden Brook.

Bank Chapel (1747)
John Wesley commemorating with a plaque sermons at Booth Bank Chapel.

This Mossway underpass is unique, in that it boasts a bench

The Paddock
Ashton Brook
M56
sp
FS
Tree
Ⓒ

Winter Hill may be visible way ahead.

Reddy Lane
Park Lane
Stamford Arms PH
Little Bollington
Scenic route (see previous page.)

Map continuation overleaf (Dunham Park)
PH

This pub is well worth the energy!
Whichever way you choose to go, try to reach the Swan, with Two Nicks before 2 p.m.; the bar food time limit.

Rostherne

Rostherne is an experience not to be missed. The shorter route along Dirty Lane is only for those in a tearing hurry to get to Dunham Park. If you want to savour the gentler pace of genuine olde worlde village life, then go thither:

There used to be four pubs in the village, but the estate landlord, fearing an invasion of lager louts and Martini marauders, closed them down. As thirsty as I was, the quiesence convinced me it wasn't such a bad thing. (The Swan on the A556 is 1½ km away — but see above.)

Mr. D. Woodbine (3, Ivy Cottages) sells line-drawings and water-colours of the village. Sign the visitors' book in the front room of his cottage. A fruitful conversation will ensue!

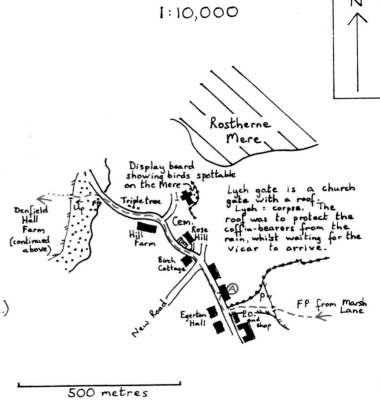

Rostherne Mere

Display board showing birds spottable on the Mere

Denfield Hall Farm (continued above)

Up

Triple tree

Cem.

Hill Farm

Rose Hill

Birch Cottage

New Road

Egerton Hall

P.O. and shop

FP from Marsh Lane

Lych gate is a church gate with a roof. Lych = corpse. The roof was to protect the coffin-bearers from the rain, whilst waiting for the vicar to arrive.

500 metres

Keeper's Cottage, on the way to Little Woolden Hall. See Map on page 32.

Warburton (Old) Church. See Map Overleaf   W. J.

Risley Moss, 2km off the main route, an old peat moss and farmland, now a nature reserve. There's an observation tower, (i), and hides. Twitchers' bliss: grey heron, owls, great spotted woodpecker, chaffinch, mallard, teal, are all residents.

Kestrels and sparrowhawks are late summer/autumn visitors.

Mersey and the Ship Canal.

Motorists pay 10p to pass the Toll Booth, above a Mersey which is no longer there.

It is said that this river claims a human sacrifice once every five years. So let's stay around just long enough to check out the moorland vista away to the north, then hurry on, over the "monstrous perfection" of the Ship Canal.

130 workmen lost their life during its construction, a 7-year long late access of Canal Fever (1890's), the purpose of which was to by-pass the heavy tax imposed on goods by the port of Liverpool.

DUNHAM PARK to GLAZEBROOK ⇌ 9 KM.

→ N

Risley Moss ↑ 2km

Dam Head Lane

Hollingreave Farm

Stile

FB

FP

Glazebrook

Chapel Lane

Barn   Track

Brook Farm

Bridge Rd.

Hollins Green

(D) At Brook Farm: cross the road, and take the cheeky-looking route across two stiles and through the yard.

CADISHEAD

MANCHESTER SHIP CANAL/MERSEY

former course of the River Mersey

Toll

Stocks and cross

WARBURTON

For Warburton Old Church: go up Wigsey Lane, beside the stocks and ruins of a cross (Cromwell's handiwork).

PARTINGTON

In the summer there are swallows, swooping acrobatically about the hedgerows and under the power lines, apparently heralding your passing by with cheeping song.

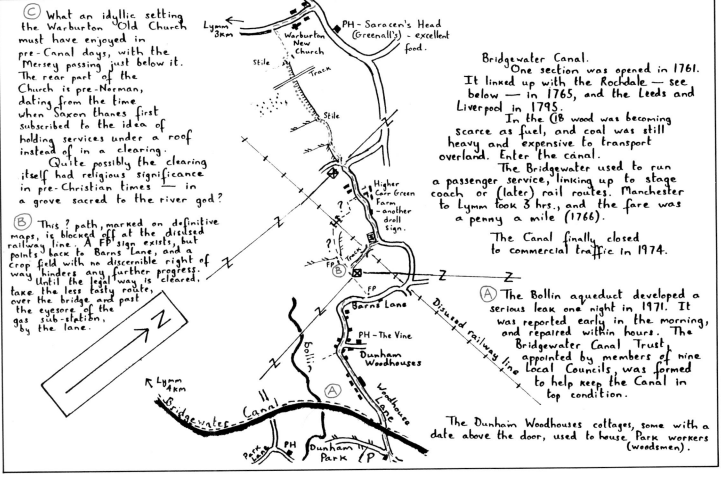

(C) What an idyllic setting the Warburton Old Church must have enjoyed in pre-Canal days, with the Mersey passing just below it. The rear part of the Church is pre-Norman, dating from the time when Saxon thanes first subscribed to the idea of holding services under a roof instead of in a clearing.

Quite possibly the clearing itself had religious significance in pre-Christian times — in a grove sacred to the river god?

(B) This ? path, marked on definitive maps, is blocked off at the disused railway line. A FP sign exists, but points back to Barns Lane, and a crop field with no discernible right of way hinders any further progress. Until the legal way is cleared, take the less tasty route, over the bridge and past the eyesore of the gas sub-station, by the lane.

Lymm 3km

PH - Saracen's Head (Greenall's) - excellent food.

Warburton New Church

Stile

Track

Stile

Higher Carr Green Farm - another droll sign.

? FP Track

? FP

Barns Lane

Disused railway line

PH - The Vine

Dunham Woodhouses

Bollin

↖ Lymm 4km

Bridgewater Canal

Woodhouse Lane

Park Lane

PH

Dunham Park P

N →

Bridgewater Canal.

One section was opened in 1761. It linked up with the Rochdale — see below — in 1765, and the Leeds and Liverpool in 1795.

In the C18 wood was becoming scarce as fuel, and coal was still heavy and expensive to transport overland. Enter the canal.

The Bridgewater used to run a passenger service, linking up to stage coach or (later) rail routes. Manchester to Lymm took 3 hrs., and the fare was a penny a mile (1766).

The Canal finally closed to commercial traffic in 1974.

(A) The Bollin aqueduct developed a serious leak one night in 1971. It was reported early in the morning, and repaired within hours. The Bridgewater Canal Trust, appointed by members of nine Local Councils, was formed to help keep the Canal in top condition.

The Dunham Woodhouses cottages, some with a date above the door, used to house Park workers (woodsmen).

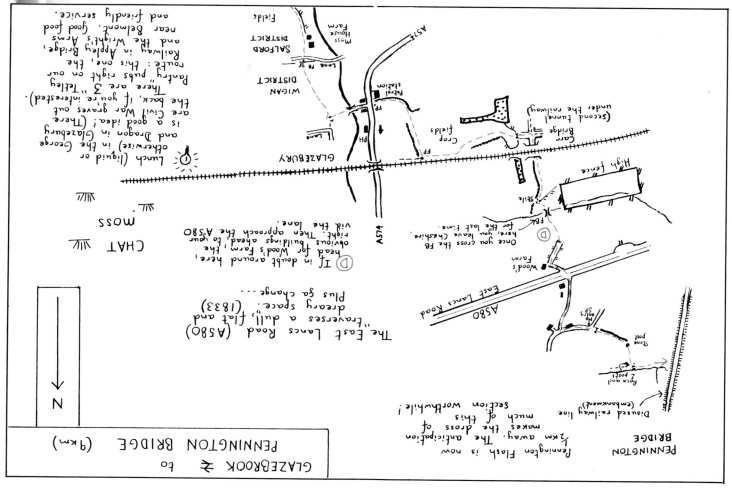

GLAZEBROOK to PENNINGTON BRIDGE (9km)

N →

CHAT MOSS

There are 3 "Telly Panfry" pubs right on our route: this one, the Railway in Appley Bridge, and the Wright's Arms near Belmont. Good food and friendly service.

Lunch (liquid or otherwise) in the George and Dragon in Glazebury (There are Civil War graves out the back, if you're interested).

GLAZEBURY

(Second tunnel under the railway)

Carr Bridge

Crop fields

Fields

SALFORD DISTRICT

Moss House Farm

WIGAN DISTRICT

Petrol station

FP

PH

Lane Fm

Lane

A574

A574

High fence

Stile

FB

Once you cross the FB here, you leave Cheshire for the last time.

The East Lancs Road (A580) "traverses a dull, flat and dreary space"...plus ça change... (1833)

If in doubt around here, head for Wood's Farm, the obvious buildings ahead to your right. Then approach the A580 via the lane.

Wood's Farm

East Lancs Road

A580

entry SP

Stone post

Rock and 2 posts

Disused railway line (embankment)

PENNINGTON BRIDGE

Pennington Flash is now ½km away. The anticipation makes the dross of much of this section worthwhile!

This isn't the most inspiring section of the GMCB, unless you're interested in farming. All is eerie silence apart from your boots squelching through the mud, and the occasional train rattling over the track.

It may help to lift the spirits if you consider the mammoth problem faced by Victorian engineers: how to lay a railway track across the spongey, quicksand-like morass of Chat Moss? Stephenson's stubbornness helps make for a stirring story: see next page.

Ⓑ Once across the M62 bridge, immediately to your left is an FP sign, apparently pointing nowhere. Cross the stile regardless, then double back along the edge of the crop field, until you reach the motorway fence. Then just follow the edge of the field, then around to the right, until you pick up the path again leading down into the woods. Cross the footbridge, and go straight up the slope, heading for the opening in the trees.

The path isn't clear across the field. Just head for the stile by the white Keeper's Cottage. Ⓒ

Ⓐ Stand on the bridge over Glaze Brook, and you are (a) dead on the GMCB —it follows the Brook for 7 km, from the Ship Canal to beyond Glazebury; (b) at the lowest point above sea level anywhere on the route (12 m.) It's a long way to Wilderness cairn, both across and up!

The dogs and geese at Great Woolden Hall are noisy, but not unfriendly. Eggs for sale.

Ducks and moorhens on the Brook may lighten the tedium of this stretch.

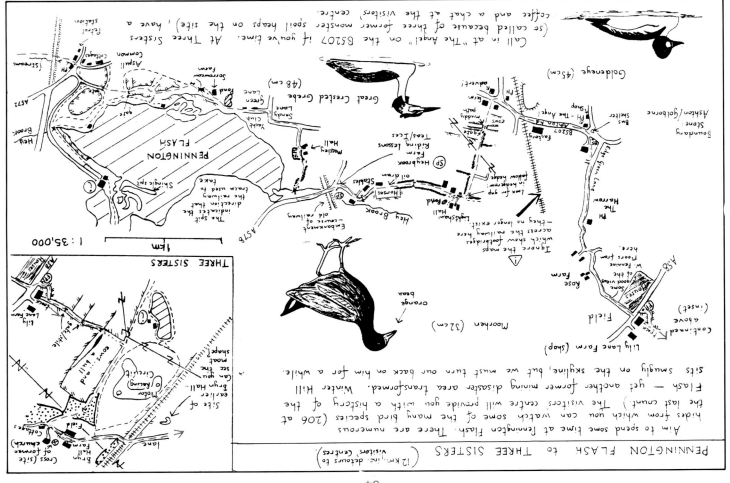

Across the Mosses: a brief History.

Prehistoric ridgeways (some of which we'll be using later) were the fastest means of travel for Stone Age man. Long before the Romans with their A to B mentality built a network of roads across Britain, high ground afforded travel unhampered by the lowland peat bogs and marshes.

The peat mosses, sullenly mobile, teeming with life (marsh-plants, waders, dragonflies, eels), quicksand-like and tending to swell in wet weather, seemed almost to be sentient creatures themselves.

This was the formidable opponent, in the shape of Chat Moss, that faced George Stephenson and his Rocket when he came to construct the Manchester-Liverpool railway line in the 1820's.

Three years of survey, drainage-ditch digging, and attempts to sink a foundation into the morass seemed to be getting nowhere slowly. Then one Robert Stannard suggested laying timber herring-bone fashion, in the form of a raft so as to spread the weight. This, together with an improvement in the foundation composition, provided the necessary firmness with pliability.

New Year's Day, 1830: the Rocket made the first rail crossing of the Moss. It was seen as a triumph over nature, by dint of ingenuity and hard graft; a Victorian morality play, perhaps.

Today, 160 years of drainage later, the peat still shudders as a train passes.

Ashurst's Beacon

BILLINGE BEACON—minus the graffiti!

R.F.

Abbey Lakes   See Map on Page 39

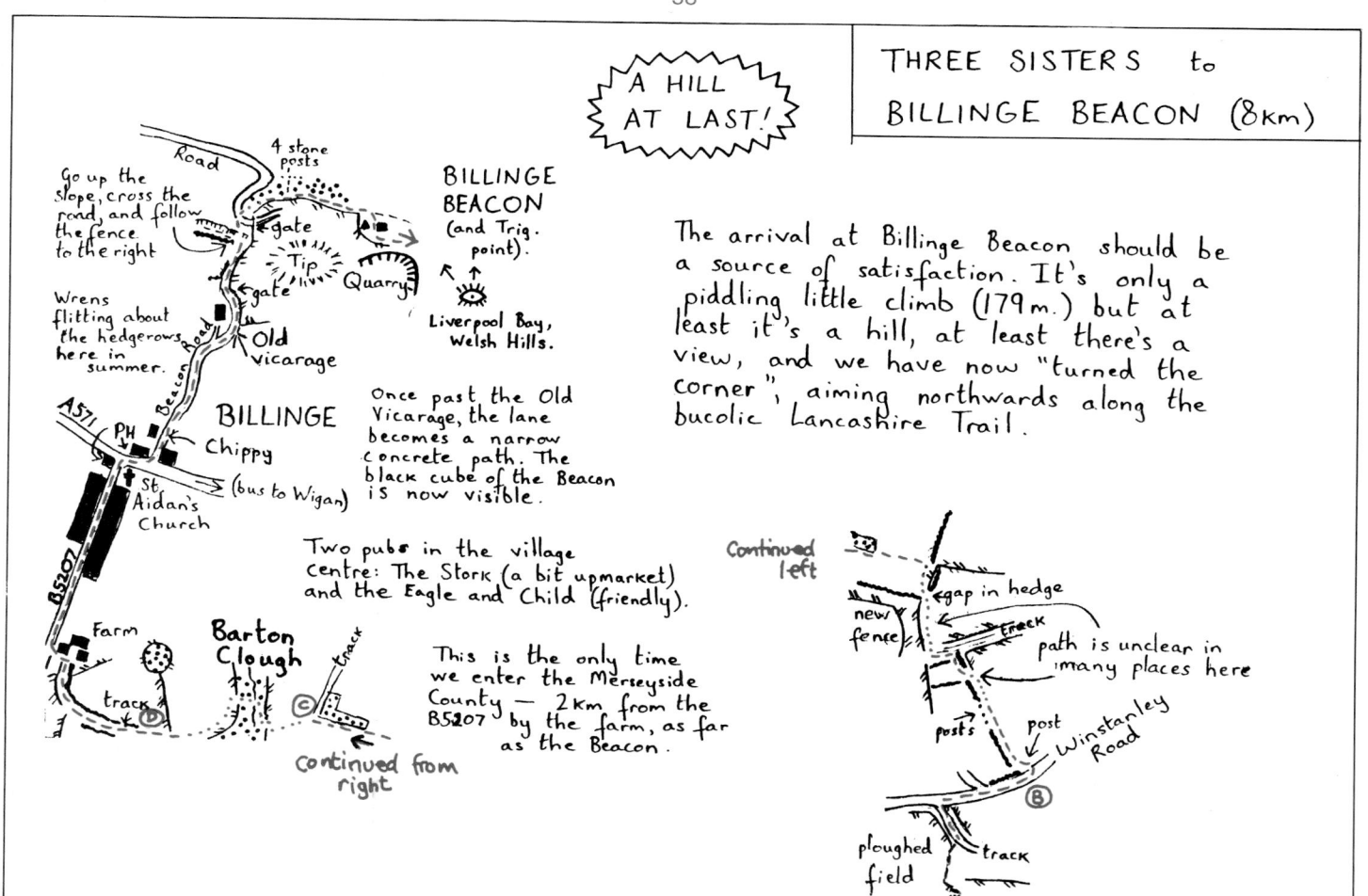

A HILL AT LAST!

THREE SISTERS to BILLINGE BEACON (8km)

The arrival at Billinge Beacon should be a source of satisfaction. It's only a piddling little climb (179 m.) but at least it's a hill, at least there's a view, and we have now "turned the corner", aiming northwards along the bucolic Lancashire Trail.

Go up the slope, cross the road, and follow the fence to the right

Road

4 stone posts

gate

Tip

gate

Quarry

BILLINGE BEACON (and Trig. point).

Liverpool Bay, Welsh Hills.

Wrens flitting about the hedgerows here in summer.

Old vicarage

Beacon Road

BILLINGE

A571

PH

Chippy

(bus to Wigan)

St. Aidan's Church

B5207

Once past the Old Vicarage, the lane becomes a narrow concrete path. The black cube of the Beacon is now visible.

Two pubs in the village centre: The Stork (a bit upmarket) and the Eagle and Child (friendly).

This is the only time we enter the Merseyside County — 2km from the B5207 by the farm, as far as the Beacon.

Farm

Barton Clough

track

C

track

Continued from right

Continued left

gap in hedge

new fence

track

path is unclear in many places here

posts

post

Winstanley Road

B

ploughed field

track

How to cross Barton Clough:

1. Head diagonally away from the corner of the L-shaped wood Ⓒ and down the field towards the Clough.

2. Cross the barbed wire fence at the two posts, then turn right, along the brook, for about 10 metres.

3. Cross the brook where there's a gap in the nettles.

4. Climb the opposite bank, and go under the wire.

5. Follow the edge of the field to your left, until you meet the track Ⓓ

⟶ N

Ⓑ On Winstanley Road, watch for the bend, and a hedgerow going across the field to your left. Look for a small gap in the hedge that runs alongside the road — the gap is marked with a post. An irritating 2km section through the farmland, dogged by fences, and almost claustrophobic. Get out onto the B5207 as soon as possible: Billinge beckons.

Ⓐ At Ryecroft Farm, turn right into the driveway, then look for a stile immediately on your left. The path goes between two wooden fences, over another stile, then between a ploughed field and an enclosure full of geese. Look for the gate into the horse field, and go over the stile. All this in the same general direction (westwards).

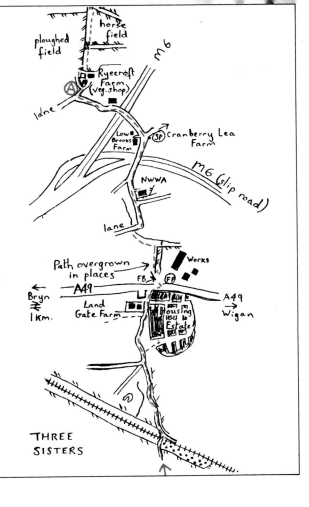

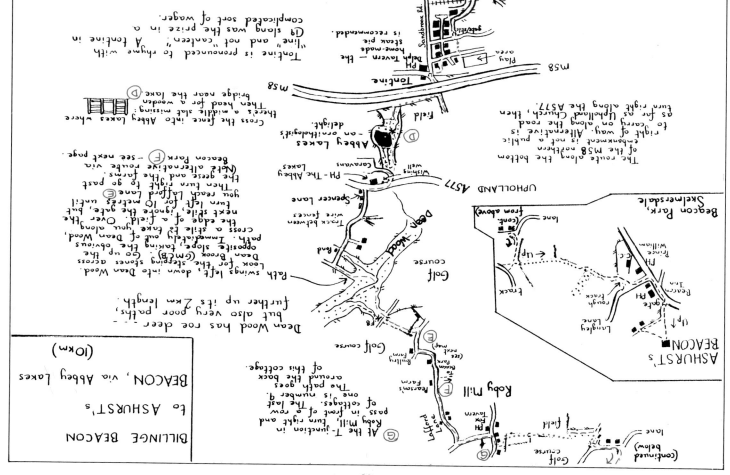

BILLINGE BEACON
to ASHURST'S
BEACON, via Abbey Lakes
(10km)

Tontine is pronounced to rhyme with 'line' and not "canteen." A tontine in a line along was the prize in a complicated sort of wager.

Delph Tavern — the home-made steak pie is recommended.

Sandbrook Rd.
Play area
M58
Tontine

Cross the fence into Abbey Lakes where there's a middle slat missing. Then head for a wooden bridge near the lake. (D)

Abbey Lakes — an ornithologist's delight.

Field

The route along the bottom of the M58 northern embankment is not a public right of way. Alternative is to carry on along the road as far as Upholland Church, then turn right along the A577.

PH – The Abbey Lakes
Caravans
Wishing well
UPHOLLAND A577
Spencer Lane
Track between wire fences

Note alternative route via the geese and the farms. Then turn right to go past Beacon Park F — see next page.

Then turn left for 10 metres until you reach Lafford Lane. (E) next stile, ignore the gate, but cross a stile to take you along the edge of a field. Over the ... obvious path. Immediately out of Dean Wood, cross a stile to field you along the opposite slope, taking the obvious Dean Brook (GmcB). Go up the Look for the stepping stones across Path swings left, down into Dean Wood.

Dean Wood has roe deer — but also very poor paths, further up its 2km length.

Dean Wood
Golf course

Beacon Park, Skelmersdale
(cont. from above)
lane
up →
track
G.C.
Prince William PH
rough track
Beacon Inn PH
gate
Up↑
Langley Lane
ASHURST'S BEACON

Roby Mill
Pearson's Farm
Beacon Park Farm (see next map)
Bullry Farm
(E)
Golf course

The path goes around the back of this cottage. The last one is number 9.

At the T-junction in Roby Mill, turn right and pass in front of a row of cottages. (G)

Lafford Lane
PH Fox Tavern
field
(continued below)
lane
Golf course

There are a number of abandoned mineshafts hereabouts, recalling the heyday of coal, when Wigan was the capital of E. Lancs, and the Lancashire pits were the third most productive in Britain, behind Northumberland/Durham and Scotland.

Look back SE before descending from the Beacon: can you see Pennington Flash?

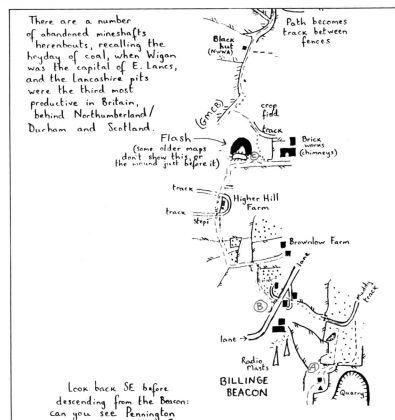

Path becomes track between fences

Black hut (NWWA)

(GMCB)

crop field

track

Flash (some older maps don't show this, or the mound just before it)

Brick works (chimneys)

E

track

track

steps

Higher Hill Farm

Brownlow Farm

lane

B

muddy track

lane →

A

Radio Masts

BILLINGE BEACON

Quarry

B

N

Ⓒ Just before the brick works, there is a low (1m.) fence with a pedestrian's gate in it. The path is easy to pick up again once alongside the flash.

Ⓑ The path follows the edge of the wood, through a couple of small wooden gates, until you reach another muddy track, that leads to Brownlow Farm. Cross the stile and turn left along the track.

Ⓐ Take any of the paths northward-ish from the Beacon, to pass by the fence corner and go straight into the woods through a new gate. When you come across a muddy track, look left and you should see a gate and a stile, and beyond them, the white and brown farmhouses.
    At the farm, the way is clearly signposted until the lane; then find the obscure path into the woods, just to the left of the private driveway. Ⓑ

Ashurst's Beacon

R.F.

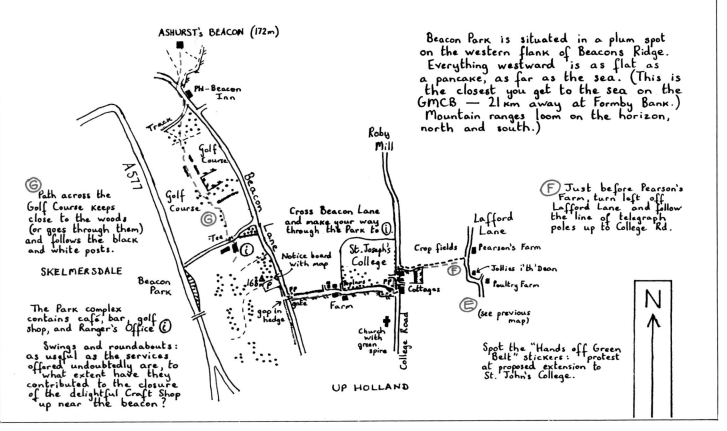

ASHURST's BEACON (172m)

PH-Beacon Inn

Track

Golf Course

A577

Golf Course

Beacon Lane

Roby Mill

Beacon Park is situated in a plum spot on the western flank of Beacons Ridge. Everything westward is as flat as a pancake, as far as the sea. (This is the closest you get to the sea on the GMCB — 21 km away at Formby Bank.) Mountain ranges loom on the horizon, north and south.)

G Path across the Golf Course keeps close to the woods (or goes through them) and follows the black and white posts.

SKELMERSDALE

G

Tee

i

Cross Beacon Lane and make your way through the Park to i

Notice board with map

St. Joseph's College

Crop fields

Lafford Lane

Pearson's Farm

F Just before Pearson's Farm, turn left off Lafford Lane and follow the line of telegraph poles up to College Rd.

Jollies i'th'Dean

F

Poultry Farm

Beacon Park

The Park complex contains café, bar, golf shop, and Ranger's Office i

Swings and roundabouts: as useful as the services offered undoubtedly are, to what extent have they contributed to the closure of the delightful Craft Shop up near the beacon?

168

gap in hedge

gate

Farm

Cottages

E (see previous map)

Church with green spire

College Road

Spot the "Hands off Green Belt" stickers: protest at proposed extension to St. John's College.

UP HOLLAND

N

ASHURST'S BEACON to STANDISH (8 km.)

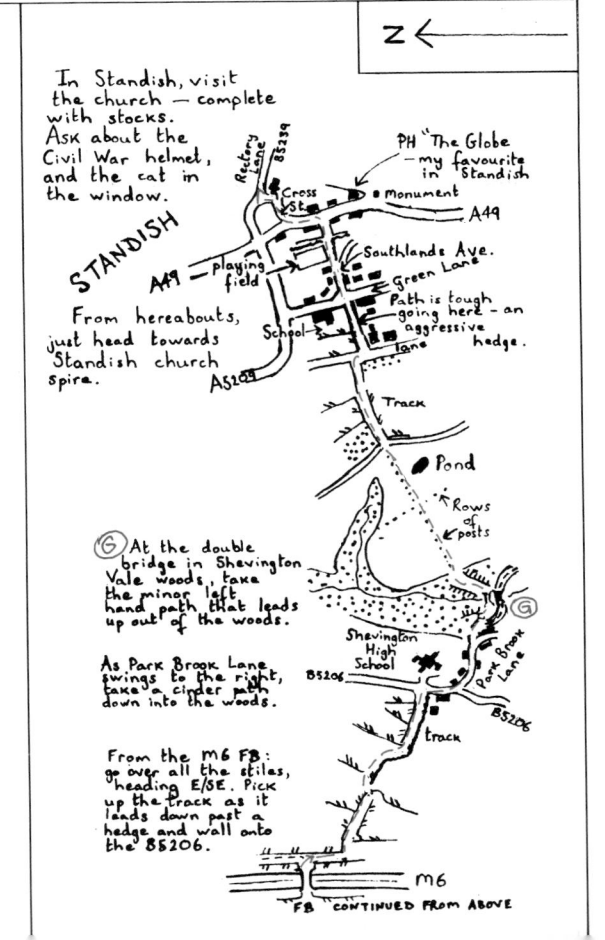

Z ←

CONTINUED IN MAP INSET BELOW

FB — a good view of Billinge/Ashurst's ridge

M6

Track

Field

Field

Field

Horses

Steps + stile

FB

Park Hey Drive

Road becomes a track

B5375

B5375

B5375

Shop/petrol station/ cottages

→ Wigan

Works

(E)

Leeds and Liverpool Canal

Appley Bridge

PH

Douglas River

Some attractive barges moored on the canal here.

PH

Concrete cylinders

Parbold 3 km

APPLEY BRIDGE (Half-way)

Cross the B5375 and head up "The Nook". Leave the track by taking a path to the left, which follows a hedgerow and a ditch (F)

Once onto the road at Appley Bridge, cross the canal bridge and turn right into Mill Lane. Just past the PH "The Water's Edge" the road narrows to pass beneath the railway bridge (E)

In Standish, visit the church — complete with stocks. Ask about the Civil War helmet, and the cat in the window.

STANDISH

Rectory Lane

B5239

Cross St.

PH "The Globe — my favourite in Standish

Monument

A49

A49

playing field

Southlands Ave.

Green Lane

Path is tough going here — an aggressive hedge.

School

Lane

A5209

From hereabouts, just head towards Standish church spire.

Track

Pond

Rows of posts

(G) At the double bridge in Shevington Vale woods, take the minor left hand path that leads up out of the woods.

As Park Brook Lane swings to the right, take a cinder path down into the woods.

Shevington High School

(G)

Park Brook Lane

B5206

track

B5206

From the M6 FB: go over all the stiles, heading E/SE. Pick up the track as it leads down past a hedge and wall onto the B5206.

M6

FB CONTINUED FROM ABOVE

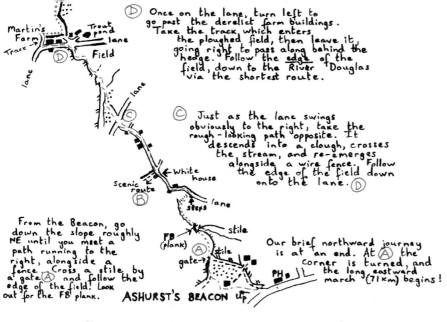

Once on the lane, turn left to go past the derelict farm buildings. Take the track which enters the ploughed field, then leave it, going right to pass along behind the hedge. Follow the edge of the field, down to the River Douglas via the shortest route.

Martin's Farm
Trout pond
lane
Track
Field
lane

C Just as the lane swings obviously to the right, take the rough-looking path opposite. It descends into a clough, crosses the stream, and re-emerges alongside a wire fence. Follow the edge of the field down onto the lane.

White house
Scenic route
B
steps
lane
FB (plank)
stile
gate
stile

From the Beacon, go down the slope roughly NE until you meet a path running to the right, alongside a fence. Cross a stile by a gate A and follow the edge of the field! Look out for the FB plank.

Our brief northward journey is at an end. At A the corner is turned, and the long eastward march (71km) begins!

PH
ASHURST'S BEACON Up

Whilst basking in the view from the Beacon, you can be deciding which route you want to take to Worthington Lakes. There is the longer, scenic route, B via Parbold Hill, Harrock Hill and Coppull Moor, as described in the excellent publication "The Lancashire Trail" (Doug Thomas et al., Hallgate Press, Wigan) — or there is the Appley Bridge — Standish route, given here. The routes join up again at Worthington Lakes.

The owner of the Craft Shop* near to Ashurst's Beacon is a mine of information about the area. This could be one of your "coffee and chat" stops. The view from the Beacon hill on a clear day is superb: Snowdonia range, Anglesey, the whole of the Lancashire coastline, and the Lakeland and Bowland fells away to the north. The Isle of Man is sometimes visible in front of a setting sun. Blackpool Tower is spottable too. Parbold Hill quarry is 3km away, almost due north. Eastwards, below that all-too familiar skyline, you can see the spire of Standish church, and due east, 9km away, the steep wooded bank of Haigh Hall Country Park. Further south, the southerly spurs of the Lancashire moors, and the Derbyshire Peaks, may also be visible.

*Craft shop was closed August 1990. I hope not for good.

The lych-gate at Standish Church

W.T.

Rivington Pike

R.F.

STANDISH to BLACKROD ⇄ 8 km

Z ←

Blackrod was the site of a Roman camp. The name means bleak or black clearing. The Romans felled many trees so as to make themselves a look-out position to see across the valley, all of which was once densely forested.

The Wandering Douglas.
The river we first met near Appley Bridge, and which eventually flows into the Ribble between Preston and the Irish Sea, starts life as a muddy spring next door to Winter Hill mast. It swings north, still a jumpable stream, by the Blackrod railway line. We meet it here on its southward journey toward Haigh Hall Lower Plantation. A tunnel carries it under Worthington Lakes. (B)

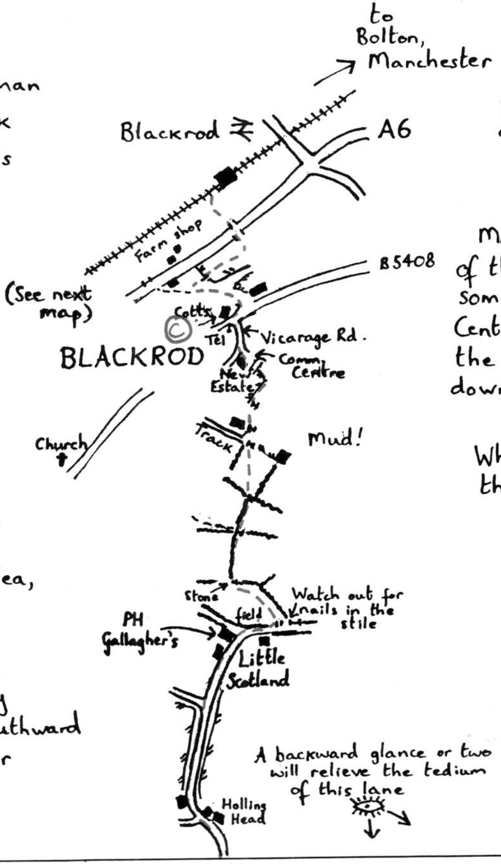

to Bolton, Manchester

Blackrod ⇄

A6

Farm shop

B5408

(See next map)

Cotts
Tel

BLACKROD

Vicarage Rd.
Comm. Centre

New Estate

Church

Track

mud!

Stone field

Watch out for snails in the stile

PH Gallagher's

Little Scotland

A backward glance or two will relieve the tedium of this lane

Holling Head

Between the cottages and the A6: either turn right to go through a gate and carry on for Blackrod ⇄; or continue bearing left, down to the A6, Lever Park and the Moors.

Make your way around the back of the new estate (not shown on some maps). Go past the Community Centre and cross the B5408 to the cottages. (C) The path continues down to the right of them.

Why "Little Scotland"? Because the hamlet lay in the centre of a mining community which employed 1,000 + migrant workers, most of them Scots. "Foreign" workers were often called Scotsmen anyway, whatever their country of origin. (Information from the bar regulars in Gallagher's. Walkers Ale appropriately recommended!)

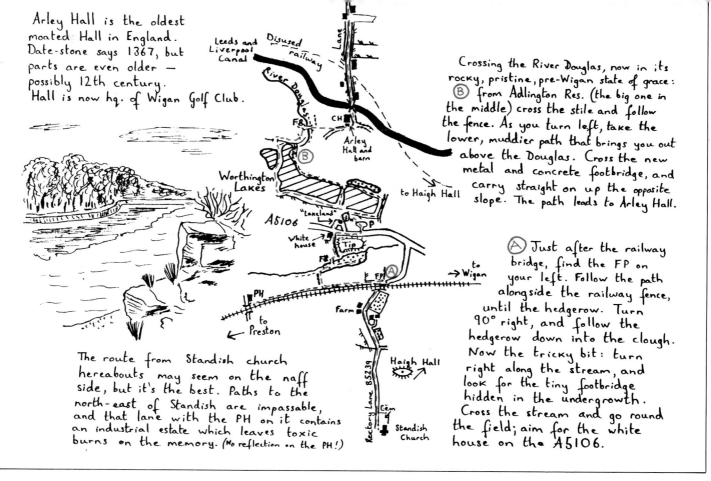

Arley Hall is the oldest moated Hall in England. Date-stone says 1367, but parts are even older — possibly 12th century. Hall is now hq. of Wigan Golf Club.

Leeds and Liverpool Canal
Disused railway
Lane
River Douglas
FB
CH
Arley Hall and barn
Ⓑ
Worthington Lakes
to Haigh Hall
A5106
"Lakeland"
P
White house
Tip
FB
FP Ⓐ
→ to Wigan
PH
Farm
to Preston →
Haigh Hall
Rectory Lane B5239
Cem
Standish Church

Crossing the River Douglas, now in its rocky, pristine, pre-Wigan state of grace: Ⓑ from Adlington Res. (the big one in the middle) cross the stile and follow the fence. As you turn left, take the lower, muddier path that brings you out above the Douglas. Cross the new metal and concrete footbridge, and carry straight on up the opposite slope. The path leads to Arley Hall.

Ⓐ Just after the railway bridge, find the FP on your left. Follow the path alongside the railway fence, until the hedgerow. Turn 90° right, and follow the hedgerow down into the clough. Now the tricky bit: turn right along the stream, and look for the tiny footbridge hidden in the undergrowth. Cross the stream and go round the field; aim for the white house on the A5106.

The route from Standish church hereabouts may seem on the naff side, but it's the best. Paths to the north-east of Standish are impassable, and that lane with the PH on it contains an industrial estate which leaves toxic burns on the memory. (No reflection on the PH!)

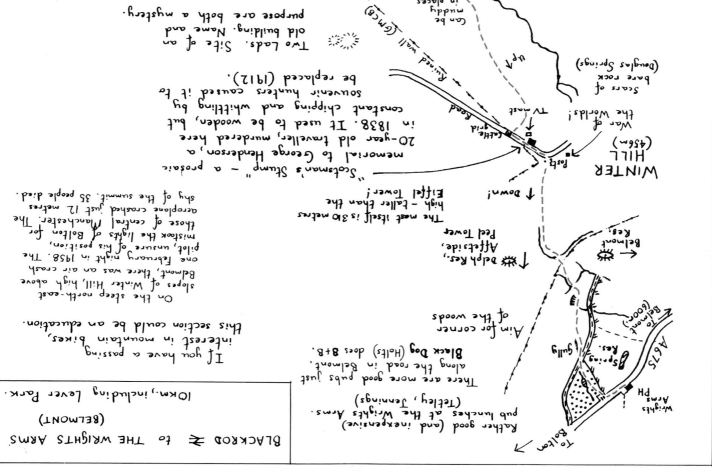

BLACKROD 🚲 to THE WRIGHTS ARMS
(BELMONT)
10km., including Lever Park.

If you have a passing interest in mountain bikes, this section could be an education.

On the steep north-east slopes of Winter Hill, high above Belmont, there was an air crash one February night in 1958. The pilot, unsure of his position, mistook the lights of Bolton for those of central Manchester. The aeroplane crashed just 12 metres shy of the summit. 35 people died.

Two Lads: Site of an old building. Name and purpose are both a mystery.

"Scotsman's Stump" – a prosaic memorial to George Henderson, a 20-year old traveller, murdered here in 1838. It used to be wooden, but constant chipping and whittling by souvenir hunters caused it to be replaced (1912).

War of the Worlds!

The mast itself is 310 metres high – taller than the Eiffel Tower!

Affetside, Peel Tower

Delph Res.

Belmont Res.

Aim for corner of the woods

Black Dog (Holts) does 8+8. There are more good pubs just along the road in Belmont.

Rather good (and inexpensive) pub lunches at the Wrights Arms. (Tetley, Jennings)

Scars of bare rock (Douglas Springs)

Ruined wall (fence)

Can be muddy in places

Up!

TV mast

Cattle grid

Posts

WINTER HILL (456m)

↑ down!

Road

↑ down!

Spring Res.

Gully

A675

(600m) Belmont

Wrights Arms PH

To Bolton

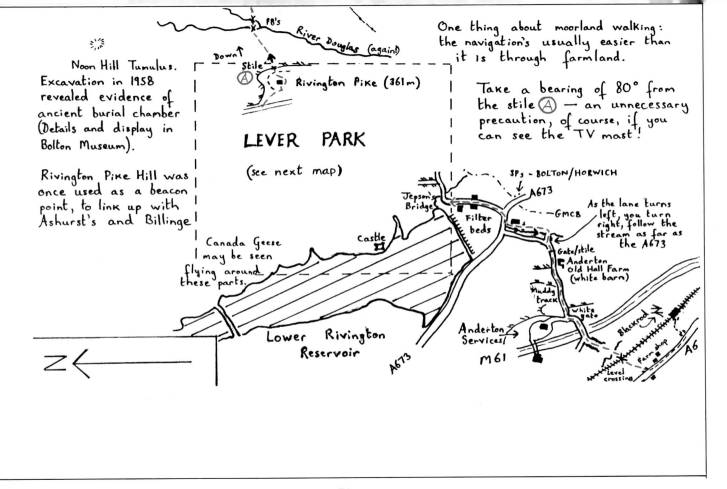

Noon Hill Tumulus. Excavation in 1958 revealed evidence of ancient burial chamber (Details and display in Bolton Museum).

Rivington Pike Hill was once used as a beacon point, to link up with Ashurst's and Billinge

One thing about moorland walking: the navigation's usually easier than it is through farmland.

Take a bearing of 80° from the stile Ⓐ — an unnecessary precaution, of course, if you can see the TV mast!

River Douglas (again!)

FB's

Down↑

Stile Ⓐ

Rivington Pike (361m)

LEVER PARK

(see next map)

Canada Geese may be seen flying around these parts.

Castle

Lower Rivington Reservoir

A673

SPs - BOLTON/HORWICH

A673

Jepson's Bridge

Filter beds

GMCB

As the lane turns left, you turn right, follow the stream as far as the A673

Gate/stile

Anderton Old Hall Farm (white barn)

Muddy track

white gate

Anderton Services

M61

Blackrod

farm shop

A6

Level crossing

N ⇐

PIGEON TOWER (DOVECOTE)   LEVER PARK

W.J.

Strawbury Duck . See Map on Page 55 .   R.F.

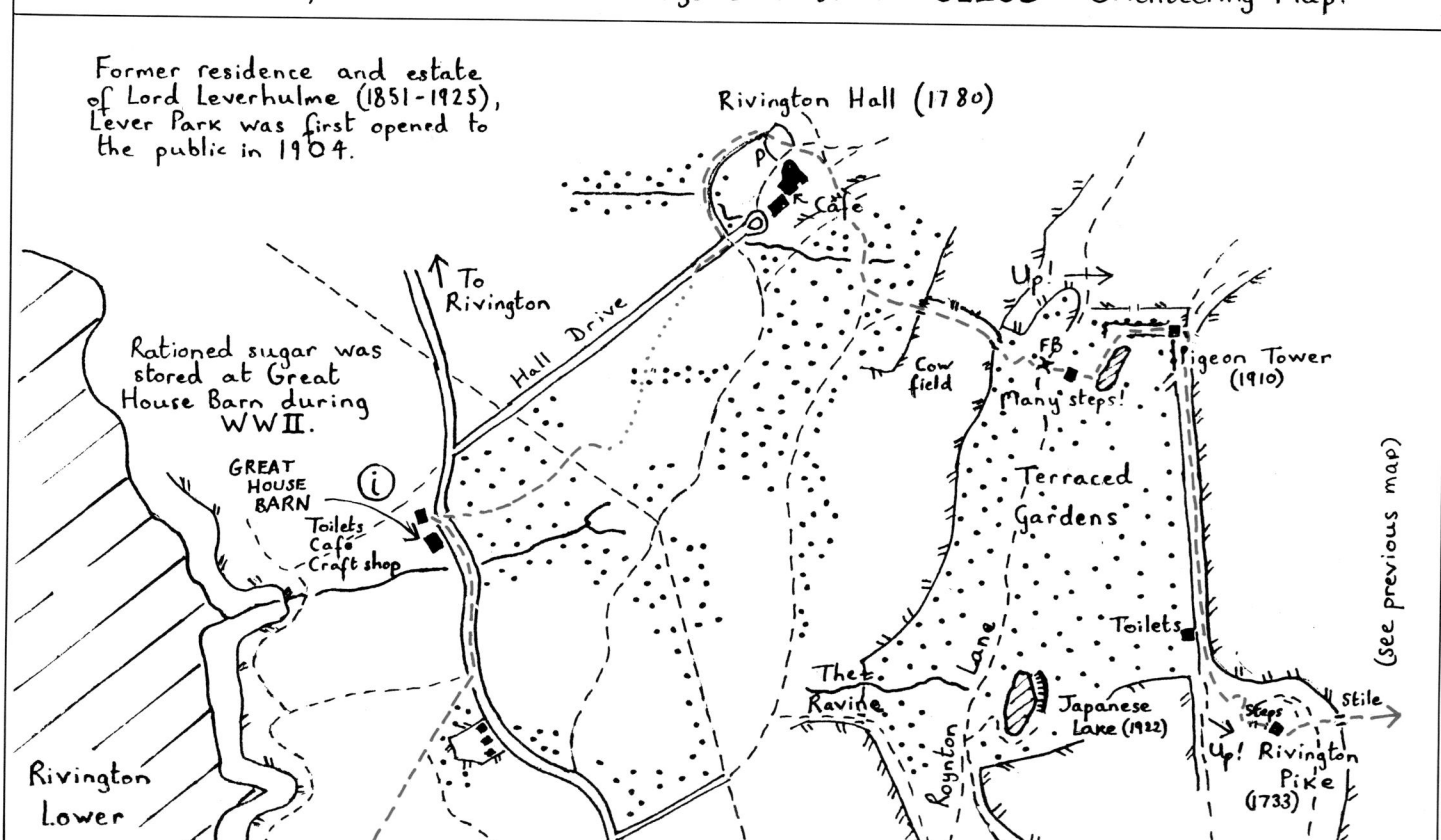

LEVER PARK, the TERRACED GARDENS and RIVINGTON PIKE
1:10,000. With acknowledgements to the SELOC Orienteering Map.

Former residence and estate of Lord Leverhulme (1851-1925), Lever Park was first opened to the public in 1904.

Rivington Hall (1780)

P

Café

To Rivington

Hall Drive

Up!

Rationed sugar was stored at Great House Barn during WWII.

Cow field

FB

Pigeon Tower (1910)

Many steps!

GREAT HOUSE BARN

i

Terraced Gardens

Toilets
Café
Craft shop

Toilets

(see previous map)

The Ravine

Roynton Lane

Japanese Lake (1922)

Steps

Stile

Up! Rivington Pike (1733)

Rivington Lower

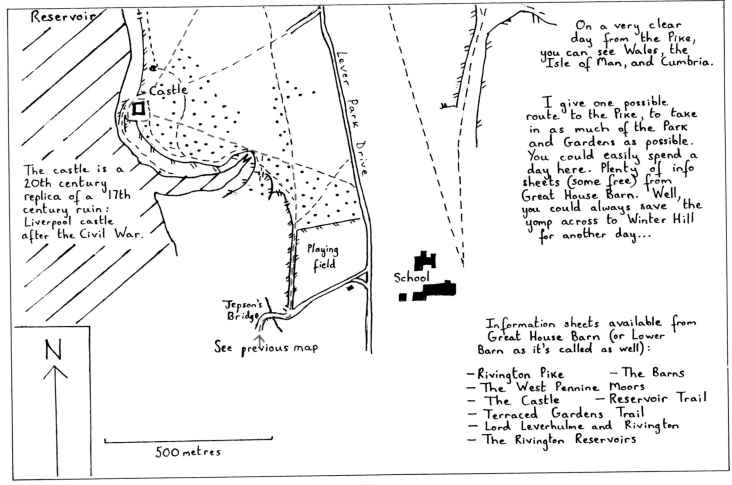

Reservoir

Castle

The castle is a 20th century replica of a 17th century ruin: Liverpool castle after the Civil War.

Lever Park Drive

Playing field

School

Jepson's Bridge

See previous map

N

500 metres

On a very clear day from the Pike, you can see Wales, the Isle of Man, and Cumbria.

I give one possible route to the Pike, to take in as much of the Park and Gardens as possible. You could easily spend a day here. Plenty of info sheets (some free) from Great House Barn. Well, you could always save the yomp across to Winter Hill for another day...

Information sheets available from Great House Barn (or Lower Barn as it's called as well):

- Rivington Pike   - The Barns
- The West Pennine Moors
- The Castle   - Reservoir Trail
- Terraced Gardens Trail
- Lord Leverhulme and Rivington
- The Rivington Reservoirs

WRIGHT'S ARMS, BELMONT to ENTWISTLE ⇄

8 km, including Yarnsdale and Fairy Battery.

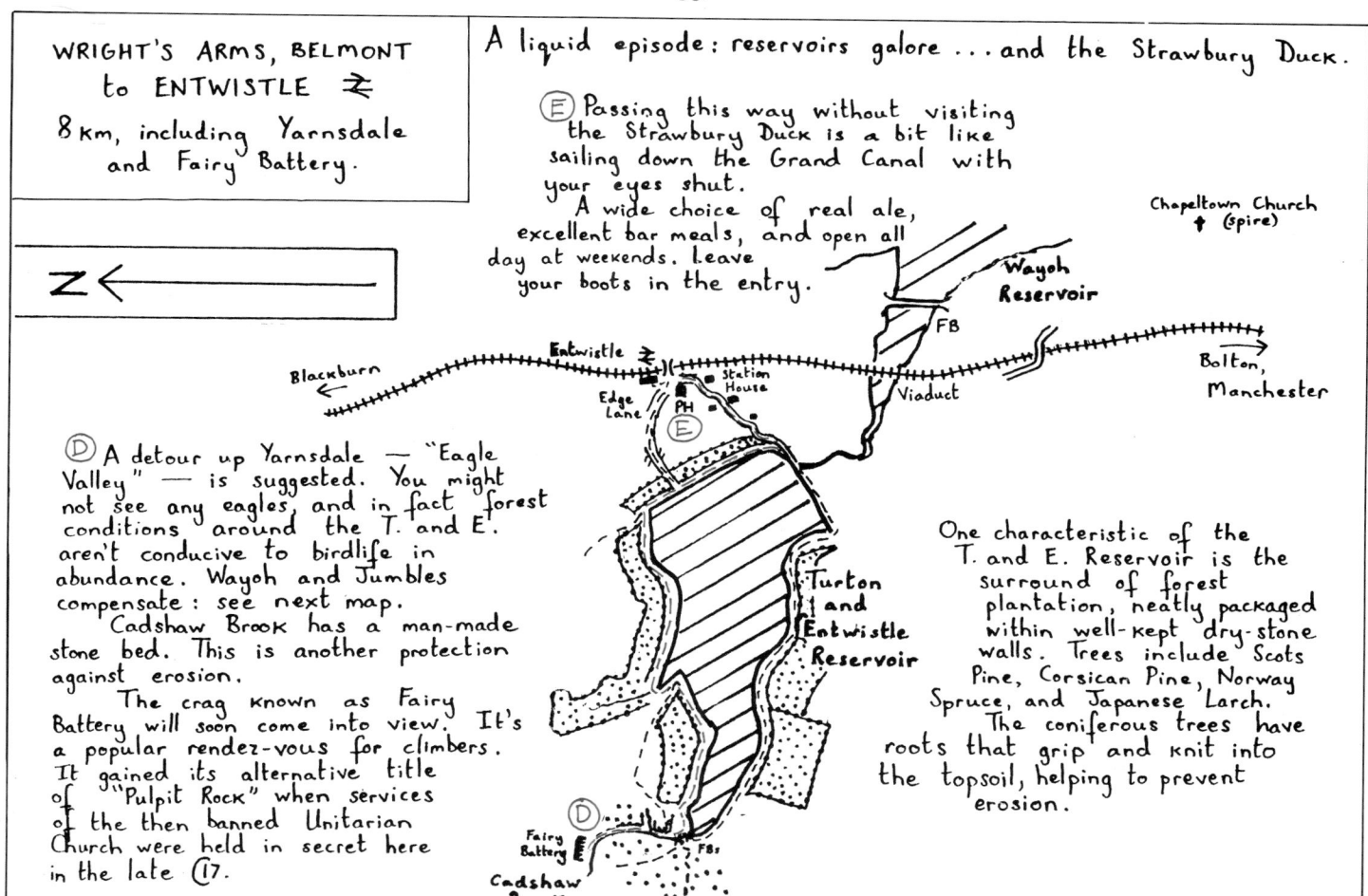

A liquid episode: reservoirs galore ... and the Strawbury Duck.

Ⓔ Passing this way without visiting the Strawbury Duck is a bit like sailing down the Grand Canal with your eyes shut.
A wide choice of real ale, excellent bar meals, and open all day at weekends. Leave your boots in the entry.

Chapeltown Church (spire)

Wayoh Reservoir

FB

Blackburn

Entwistle ⇄

Edge Lane

Station House

PH

Ⓔ

Viaduct

Bolton, Manchester

Ⓓ A detour up Yarnsdale — "Eagle Valley" — is suggested. You might not see any eagles, and in fact forest conditions around the T. and E. aren't conducive to birdlife in abundance. Wayoh and Jumbles compensate: see next map.
Cadshaw Brook has a man-made stone bed. This is another protection against erosion.
The crag known as Fairy Battery will soon come into view. It's a popular rendez-vous for climbers. It gained its alternative title of "Pulpit Rock" when services of the then banned Unitarian Church were held in secret here in the late ⑰

Turton and Entwistle Reservoir

One characteristic of the T. and E. Reservoir is the surround of forest plantation, neatly packaged within well-kept dry-stone walls. Trees include Scots Pine, Corsican Pine, Norway Spruce, and Japanese Larch.
The coniferous trees have roots that grip and knit into the topsoil, helping to prevent erosion.

Ⓓ

Fairy Battery Ⓔ

FB₁

Cadshaw Brook

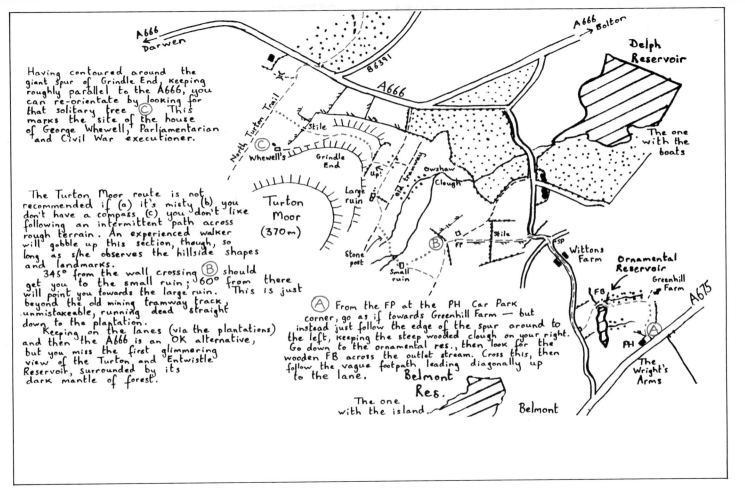

Having contoured around the giant spur of Grindle End, keeping roughly parallel to the A666, you can re-orientate by looking for that solitary tree ©. This marks the site of the house of George Whewell, Parliamentarian and Civil War executioner.

The Turton Moor route is not recommended if (a) it's misty (b) you don't have a compass (c) you don't like following an intermittent path across rough terrain. An experienced walker will gobble up this section, though, so long as s/he observes the hillside shapes and landmarks.

345° from the wall crossing ® should get you to the small ruin; 60° from there will point you towards the large ruin. This is just beyond the old mining tramway track, unmistakeable, running dead straight down to the plantation.

Keeping on the lanes (via the plantations) and then the A666 is an OK alternative, but you miss the first glimmering view of the Turton and Entwistle Reservoir, surrounded by its dark mantle of forest.

A666 Darwen

A666 Bolton

B6391

A666

Delph Reservoir

The one with the boats

North Turton Trail

Stile

© Whewell's

Grindle End

Turton Moor (370m)

Large ruin

Up!

Owshaw Clough

Stone post

Small ruin

® FP

Stile

FSP

Wittons Farm

Ornamental Reservoir

Greenhill Farm

A675

FB

Ⓐ From the FP at the PH Car Park corner, go as if towards Greenhill Farm — but instead just follow the edge of the spur around to the left, keeping the steep wooded clough on your right. Go down to the ornamental res., then look for the wooden FB across the outlet stream. Cross this, then follow the vague footpath leading diagonally up to the lane.

PH

The Wright's Arms

Belmont Res.

The one with the island

Belmont

ENTWISTLE ⇄ to THE PACK HORSE, AFFETSIDE   9km – via Turton Tower and Jumbles Res.

Affetside and the Roman Road.

Rumour has it that the hamlet's name is derived from "Half-at-side", meaning that it was a half-way post between Manchester and Blackburn, using Watling Street.

Another item of interest is Ⓖ the headless cross. It is known as either the Old Roman Cross or the Market Cross, and historians differ as to its true origins.

In the Pack Horse (Hydes), a ⒸⒾⒾⒾ coach inn, ask about the skull, which used to be kept in a glass case above the bar. The tale may have an eerie familiarity.

Remember the A556 near Rostherne? That was the Deva (Chester) to Mancunium (M/cR) stretch of Watling St. The section that passes through Affetside was a straight route between Mancunium and Bremetennacum (Ribchester).

I had been walking alongside Jumbles for all of a minute when I was treated to the sight of a heron with its slow wing-beat, flying its silent way towards the quarry. Parts of Wayoh and Jumbles are conservation areas. Details of the rich variety of flora and fauna from the leaflet "The Jumbles Trail" and the "JET" sheets. Call in at Ⓘ.

Ⓔ After 250 metres on the A676, there is a renovated stone-wall cottage on the left. Follow the track/lane that goes up by it, and keep on this as it turns left and approaches the northerly buildings of Harry Fold Farm Ⓕ. Go through two stiles, then use the sleeve of woodland to help navigate up the hill. Cross more stiles and emerge by cow barns and a handsome cottage onto Watling Street.

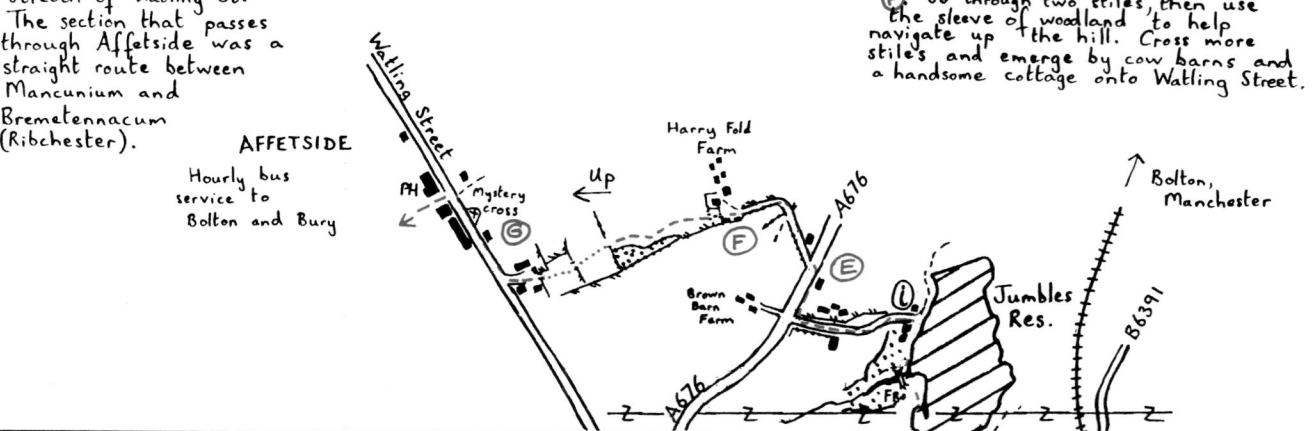

AFFETSIDE

Hourly bus service to Bolton and Bury

Watling Street · PH · Ⓖ Mystery cross · Up · Harry Fold Farm · Ⓕ · Ⓔ · A676 · Brown Barn Farm · Ⓘ · Jumbles Res. · Bolton, Manchester · B6391 · A676

Turton Towers has a chequered history, reflected perhaps by the amalgam of architecture. The (15 pele Tower was built for defence against possible invasion by the Scots. The late (16 saw the addition of the half-timbered annexes. The museum has Civil War weaponry, suits of armour and period furniture. There are also two skulls in a glass case, and the story behind why they are there is a commonly heard folk tale.

Ⓑ From the Black Bull PH: turn right and go along Bolton Rd. After about 500 metres, watch out for Birches Rd. on your left, just before the Spread Eagle. As Birches Rd turns left, take the private-looking path on your right, beyond a white gate. This leads to a FB and the first of two crossings of Bradshaw Brook.
After the FB, go left down a cobbled street, which ends at another bridge across the Brook, at right-angles to the first. Locate the FP and the path that continues by the side of Bradshaw Brook: this leads eventually to Jumbles.

Ⓐ From the Strawbury Duck: cross the railway bridge and follow the lane. 50 metres after it curves to the right, look for a stile on your left. Cross the sheep field, cross another stile and follow the twisting path down into the woods. You go beneath a rusty frame: this was part of the pulley and cable system that linked Entwistle Station with Know Mill, an old bleachworks whose ruins lie beneath the waters of the smaller northern section of Wayoh. Emerge from the woods, cross the two FBs, then turn right to follow the clear path that runs alongside the Res.

The owners of Turton Estate sold land to the railway company (1845) on condition that the bridges and any construction on the Estate wouldn't be an eyesore.

Horrobin Lane Ⓓ

Norman-style railway bridge Ⓒ

Turton Towers

Chapeltown

Bradshaw Brook

Turton Bottoms

Wayoh Res.

Viaduct

Turton and Entwistle Res.

The Norman-style railway
bridge close by Turton Towers.
W. J.
(See map on previous page) .-

Turton Towers.   R.F.

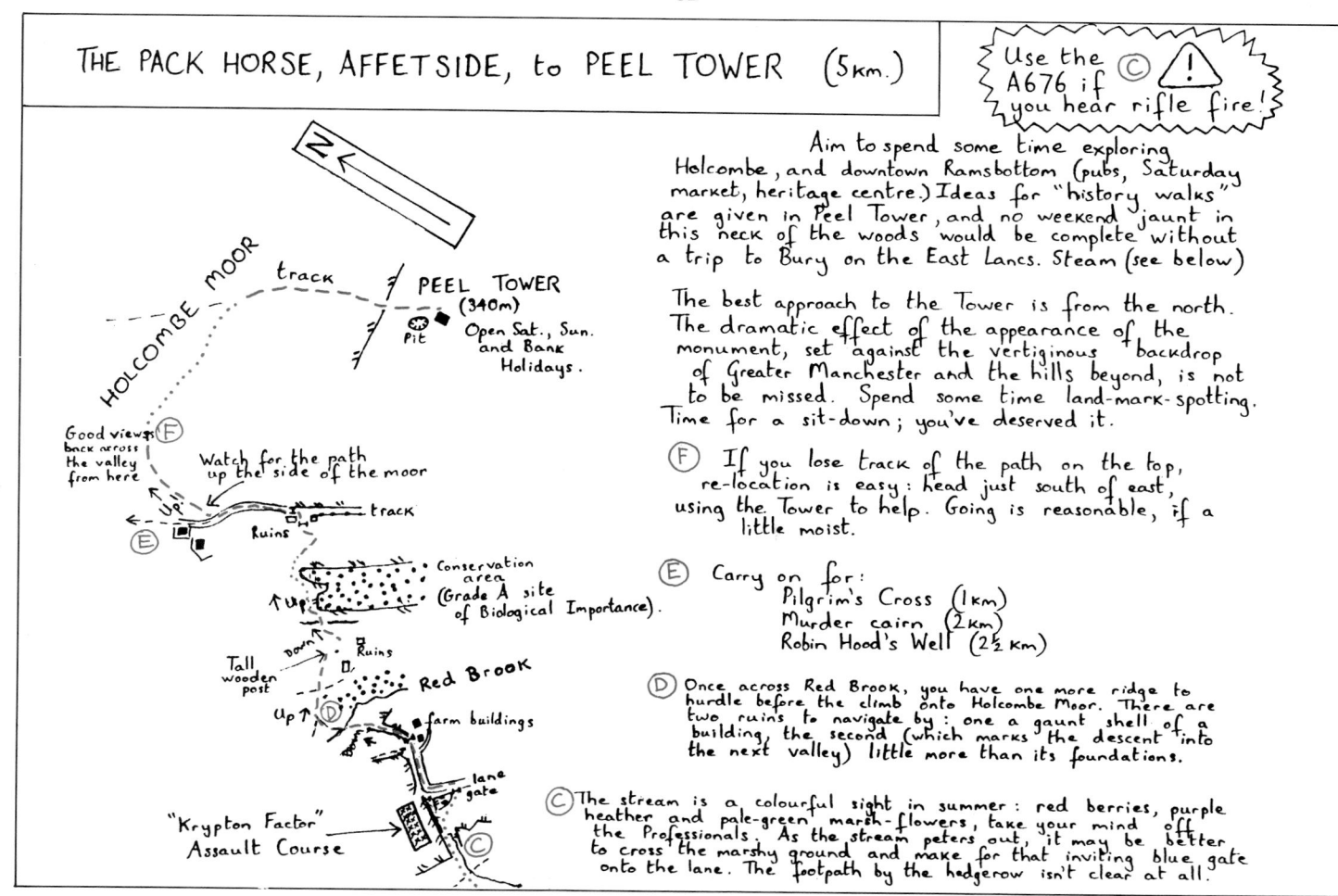

THE PACK HORSE, AFFETSIDE, to PEEL TOWER (5km.)

Use the A676 if you hear rifle fire! Ⓒ ⚠

N ↙

HOLCOMBE MOOR

track

PEEL TOWER (340m)
Open Sat., Sun. and Bank Holidays.

Pit

Good views back across the valley from here Ⓕ

Watch for the path up the side of the moor

←Up↑ Ⓔ ▦ Ruins

track

Conservation area (Grade A site of Biological Importance).

↑Up↑

Tall wooden post

Down→ Ruins

Red Brook

Up↑ Ⓓ

farm buildings

lane gate Ⓒ

"Krypton Factor" Assault Course →

Aim to spend some time exploring Holcombe, and downtown Ramsbottom (pubs, Saturday market, heritage centre.) Ideas for "history walks" are given in Peel Tower, and no weekend jaunt in this neck of the woods would be complete without a trip to Bury on the East Lancs. Steam (see below)

The best approach to the Tower is from the north. The dramatic effect of the appearance of the monument, set against the vertiginous backdrop of Greater Manchester and the hills beyond, is not to be missed. Spend some time land-mark-spotting. Time for a sit-down; you've deserved it.

Ⓕ If you lose track of the path on the top, re-location is easy: head just south of east, using the Tower to help. Going is reasonable, if a little moist.

Ⓔ Carry on for:
Pilgrim's Cross (1km)
Murder cairn (2km)
Robin Hood's Well (2½ km)

Ⓓ Once across Red Brook, you have one more ridge to hurdle before the climb onto Holcombe Moor. There are two ruins to navigate by: one a gaunt shell of a building, the second (which marks the descent into the next valley) little more than its foundations.

Ⓒ The stream is a colourful sight in summer: red berries, purple heather and pale-green marsh-flowers, take your mind off the Professionals. As the stream peters out, it may be better to cross the marshy ground and make for that inviting blue gate onto the lane. The footpath by the hedgerow isn't clear at all.

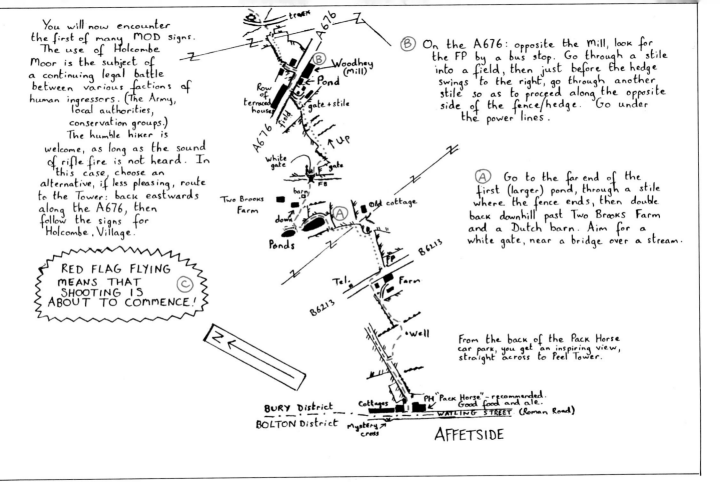

You will now encounter the first of many MOD signs. The use of Holcombe Moor is the subject of a continuing legal battle between various factions of human ingressors. (The Army, local authorities, conservation groups.)

The humble hiker is welcome, as long as the sound of rifle fire is not heard. In this case, choose an alternative, if less pleasing, route to the Tower: back eastwards along the A676, then follow the signs for Holcombe Village.

RED FLAG FLYING MEANS THAT SHOOTING IS ABOUT TO COMMENCE! ©

Ⓑ On the A676: opposite the mill, look for the FP by a bus stop. Go through a stile into a field, then just before the hedge swings to the right, go through another stile so as to proceed along the opposite side of the fence/hedge. Go under the power lines.

Ⓐ Go to the far end of the first (larger) pond, through a stile where the fence ends, then double back downhill past Two Brooks Farm and a Dutch barn. Aim for a white gate, near a bridge over a stream.

From the back of the Pack Horse car park, you get an inspiring view, straight across to Peel Tower.

PH "Pack Horse" - recommended. Good food and ale.

track
A676
Ⓑ Woodhey (Mill)
Pond
Row of terraced houses
A676
field
gate + stile
↑ UP
white gate
gate
FB
barn
Two Brooks Farm
down
Ⓐ
Old cottage
Ponds
FP
B6213
Tel.
Farm
B6213
•well
Cottages
BURY District
BOLTON District
Mystery cross
PH
WATLING STREET (Roman Road)
AFFETSIDE
N

PEEL TOWER, looking NE, towards Scout Moor.

The Tower was completed in 1852, and re-opened to the public in 1985. It's 40 metres high.

An austere monument (Victoriana resilient) to Sir Robert Peel. Pay your pittance and mount the narrow stairway — the third one to be installed — to emerge on an open balustrade, where the wild air will greet you. The views rival, if not surpass, those afforded by Rivington Pike. We're too far inland for a shoreline to draw the eye, but the 360° sweep more than compensates.

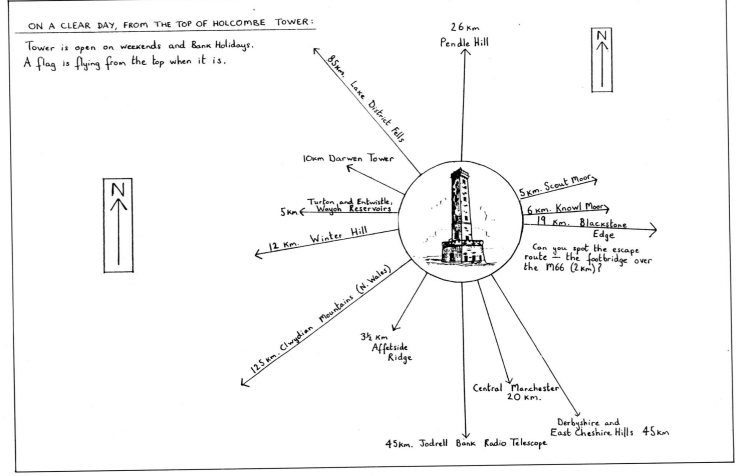

Tower is open on weekends and Bank Holidays.
A flag is flying from the top when it is.

26 Km
Pendle Hill

N

85km. Lake District Fells

10km Darwen Tower

5 Km. Scout Moor

Turton and Entwistle, Wayoh Reservoirs
5 km ←

6 Km. Knowl Moor

19 Km. Blackstone Edge

12 Km. Winter Hill

Can you spot the escape route — the footbridge over the M66 (2 km)?

N

125 Km. Clwydian mountains (N. Wales)

3½ Km Affetside Ridge

Central Marchester 20 Km.

Derbyshire and East Cheshire Hills 45 Km

45km. Jodrell Bank Radio Telescope

In 1986 the MOD announced its intention to annex an extra 916 acres of Holcombe Moor, eastwards towards Peel Tower, for Army exercises. It stated that this would not restrict public access, and that no live ammunition would be used on the newly-acquired land.

Conservation groups and local authorities protested about possible noise, and disturbance to wild life. A public enquiry was held in October 1989. A total of 55 witnesses were heard.

The latest state of play (Feb. '91) has a touch of Catch-22 about it. The MOD has bought the said land, but are now awaiting permission to use it!

This one seems destined to run and run.

Holcombe Village protest, 1988.

(Photo taken from "Countryside and Wildlife in Greater Manchester", Summer 1988.)

Cheesden Lumb Mill
See map on Page 70

W.J.

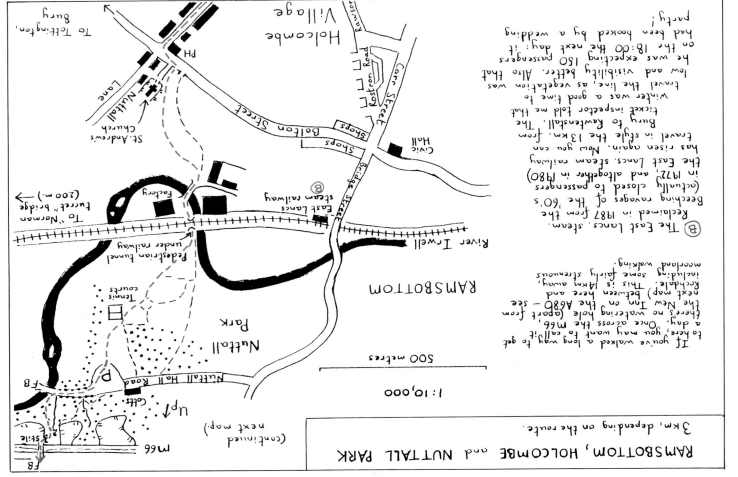

Runs weekends and Bank Holidays.
Association of Railway Preservation
Societies' Award 1987.

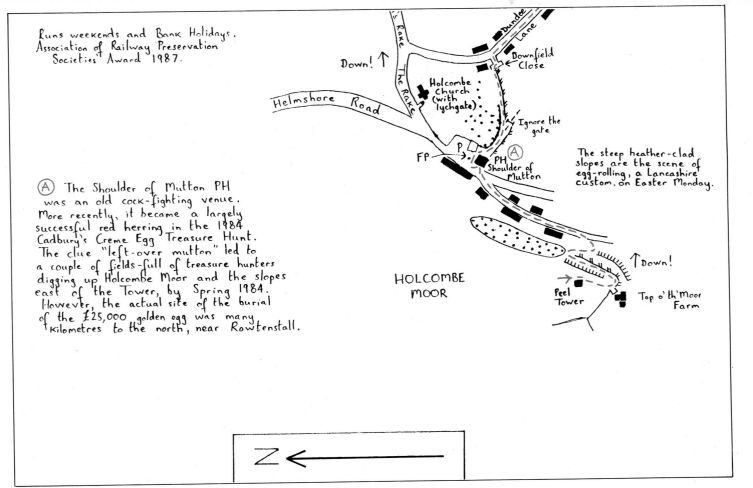

(A) The Shoulder of Mutton PH
was an old cock-fighting venue.
More recently, it became a largely
successful red herring in the 1984
Cadbury's Creme Egg Treasure Hunt.
The clue "left-over mutton" led to
a couple of fields-full of treasure hunters
digging up Holcombe Moor and the slopes
east of the Tower, by Spring 1984.
However, the actual site of the burial
of the £25,000 golden egg was many
kilometres to the north, near Rowtenstall.

Down! ↑

Holcombe
Church
(with
lychgate)

Helmshore Road

Ignore the
gate

The steep heather-clad
slopes are the scene of
egg-rolling, a Lancashire
custom, on Easter Monday.

Dundee Lane

Downfield
Close

FP   P.
         PH
         Shoulder of
         Mutton (A)

HOLCOMBE
MOOR

↑Down!

Peel
Tower

Top o'th'moor
Farm

N ←

NUTTALL PARK to HEALEY DELL, via "The Forgotten Valley" and Rooley Moor (12km)   COMPASS!

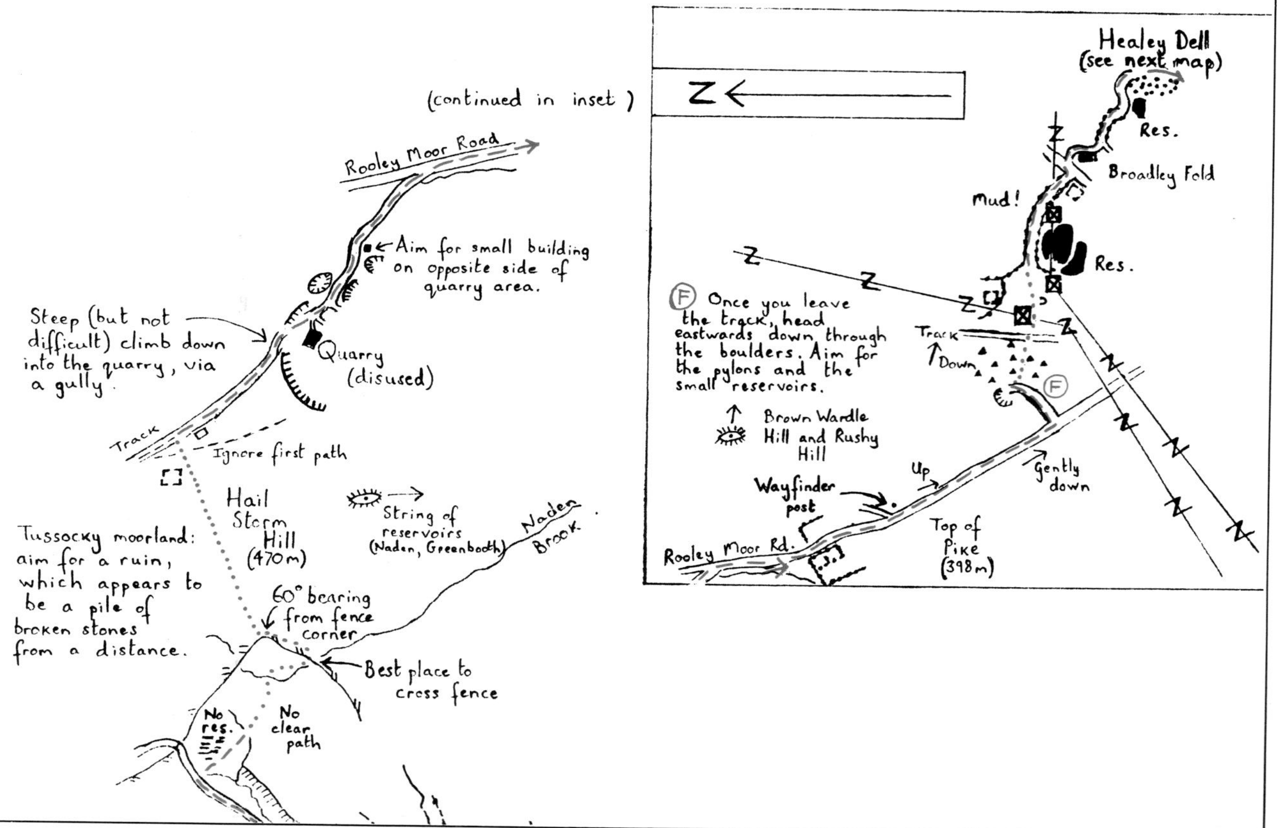

N →

Top of Pike (398m)

Rooley Moor Rd.

Wa_finder post

Brown Wardle Hill and Rushy Hill

gently down

Up

Down

Track

small reservoirs.

(F) Once you leave the track, head eastwards down through the boulders. Aim for the pylons and the small reservoirs.

Res.

Broadley Fold

Res.

mud!

Healey Dell (see next map)

Steep (but not difficult) climb down into the quarry, via a gully.

Quarry (disused)

Aim for small building on opposite side of quarry area.

Rooley Moor Road

(continued in inset)

Track

Ignore first path.

Naden Brook

String of reservoirs (Naden, Greenbooth)

Hail Storm Hill (470m)

Tussocky moorland: aim for a ruin, which appears to be a pile of broken stones from a distance.

60° bearing from fence corner.

Best place to cross fence

No clear path

No Res

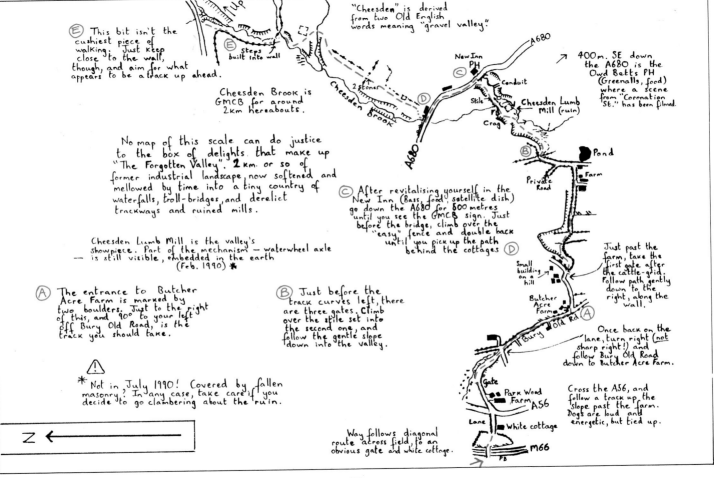

E This bit isn't the cushiest piece of walking. Just keep close to the wall, though, and aim for what appears to be a track up ahead.

E steps built into wall

UP

"Cheesden" is derived from two Old English words meaning "gravel valley"

A680

New Inn PH

C

Conduit

Cheesden Lumb Mill (ruin)

Stile

Crag

400m. SE down the A680 is the Owd Betts PH (Greenalls, food) where a scene from "Coronation St." has been filmed.

Cheesden Brook is GMCB for around 2km hereabouts.

2 stones

Cheesden Brook

A680

D

No map of this scale can do justice to the box of delights that make up "The Forgotten Valley". 2 km. or so of former industrial landscape, now softened and mellowed by time into a tiny country of waterfalls, troll-bridges, and derelict trackways and ruined mills.

C After revitalising yourself in the New Inn (Bass, food, satellite dish) go down the A680 for 500 metres until you see the GMCB sign. Just before the bridge, climb over the "easy" fence and double back until you pick up the path behind the cottages

B

Pond

Farm

Private Road

D

Cheesden Lumb Mill is the valley's showpiece. Part of the mechanism — waterwheel axle — is still visible, embedded in the earth (Feb. 1990) *

Small building on a hill

Butcher Acre Farm

A

Just past the farm, take the first gate after the cattle-grid. Follow path gently down to the right, along the wall.

A The entrance to Butcher Acre Farm is marked by two boulders. Just to the right of this, and 90° to your left off Bury Old Road, is the track you should take.

B Just before the track curves left, there are three gates. Climb over the stile set into the second one, and follow the gentle slope down into the valley.

Bury Old Rd.

Once back on the lane, turn right (not sharp right!) and follow Bury Old Road down to Butcher Acre Farm.

⚠️

Gate

Park Wood Farm

A56

* Not in, July 1990! Covered by fallen masonry? In any case, take care if you decide to go clambering about the ruin.

Lane

White cottage

Cross the A56, and follow a track up the slope past the farm. Dogs are loud and energetic, but tied up.

M66

FB

Way follows diagonal route across field, to an obvious gate and white cottage.

Z ←

the Dell is another disused railway line (opened 1870, closed 1967).

The main pathway through

LANCASHIRE (Rossendale)

A671

FB

Res

Broadley Fold

GREATER MANCHESTER (Rochdale)

Oakenshaw Ave.

FB

GMC8 River — (follows Spodden as far as (A))

N

1:10,000.

Viaduct, Visitors' Centre, Mills.
Robin Hood's Well (again!)
Birds you may see: swifts and martins,
darting across the steep valley below
the viaduct;
Woodpeckers and jays
fussing around in the woods;
dippers (they look a bit
like wrens) plunging into the river for
insects.

HEALEY DELL - a detour - 2½ km.

"Don't leave anything but footprints
Don't take anything but photographs
Don't kill anything but time"
—from "The Healey Dell Nature
Trail", a leaflet published by Groundwork.

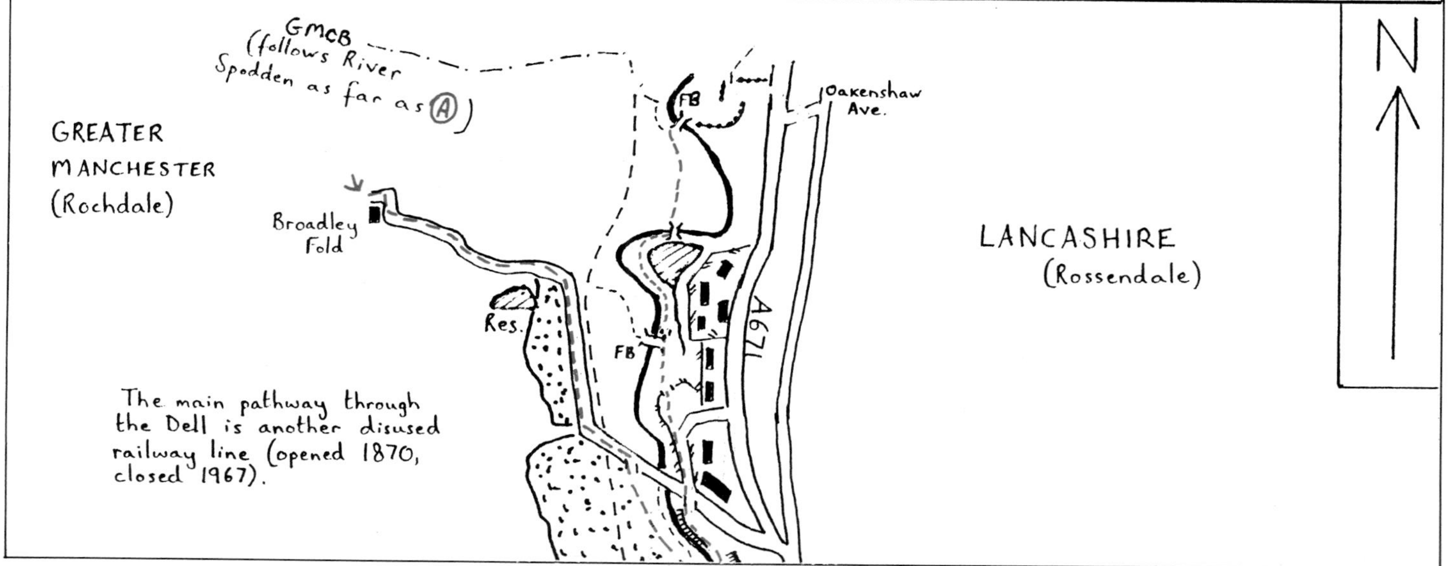

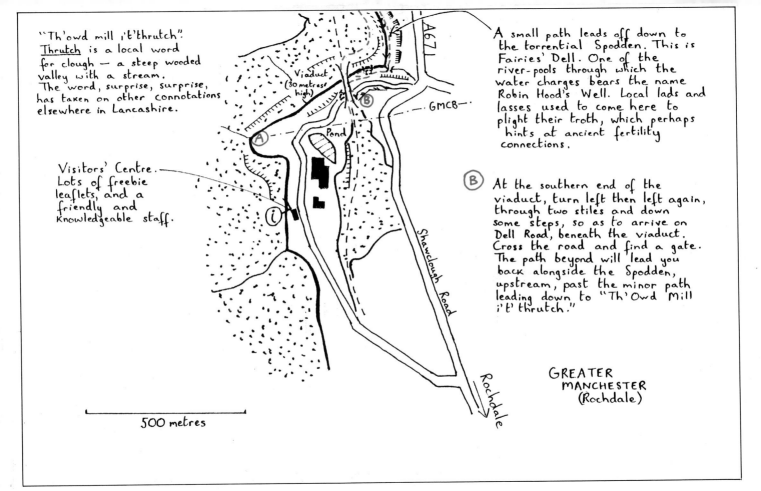

"Th'owd mill i't'thrutch". _Thrutch_ is a local word for clough — a steep wooded valley with a stream. The word, surprise, surprise, has taken on other connotations elsewhere in Lancashire.

Visitors' Centre. Lots of freebie leaflets, and a friendly and knowledgeable staff.

Viaduct (30 metres high)

Pond

GMCB

A671

Shawclough Road

Rochdale

A small path leads off down to the torrential Spodden. This is Fairies' Dell. One of the river-pools through which the water charges bears the name Robin Hood's Well. Local lads and lasses used to come here to plight their troth, which perhaps hints at ancient fertility connections.

B At the southern end of the viaduct, turn left then left again, through two stiles and down some steps, so as to arrive on Dell Road, beneath the viaduct. Cross the road and find a gate. The path beyond will lead you back alongside the Spodden, upstream, past the minor path leading down to "Th'Owd Mill i't' thrutch."

GREATER MANCHESTER (Rochdale)

500 metres

North-east of Watergrove Reservoir; see next map.

Cross the ford by the cairn (SE of Crook Hill), go up the next slope — Turn Slack Hill — and:

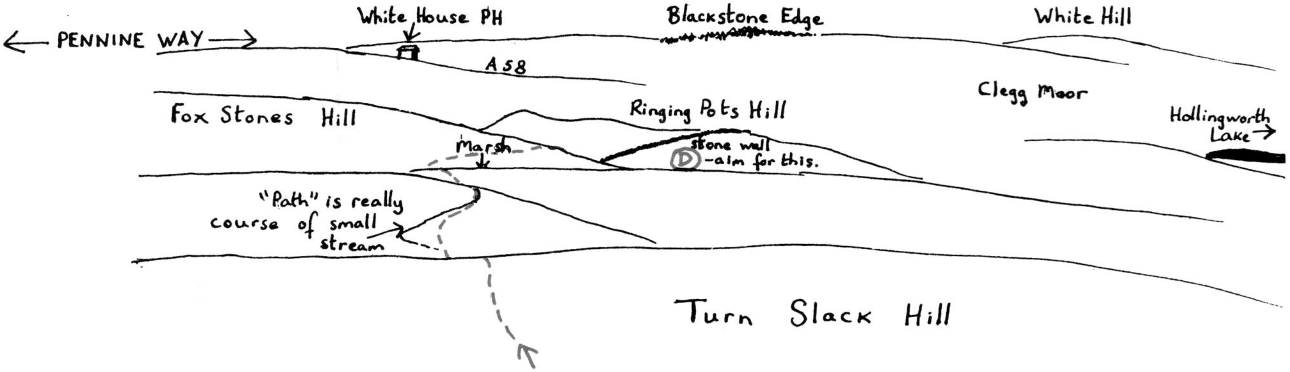

← PENNINE WAY →

White House PH

Blackstone Edge

White Hill

A58

Fox Stones Hill

Ringing Pots Hill

Clegg Moor

Hollingworth Lake →

Marsh

stone wall
—aim for this.

D

"Path" is really
course of small
stream →

Turn Slack Hill

St. Bartholomew's

Church,

Whitworth

"Wall of History". Before the village of Watergrove was submerged by the reservoir waters, several date- and name-stones were salvaged.

Pasture House. As you approach the farmhouses, you will see a blue gate in the wall on your right. Go through this, then cross the gate leading onto the driveway. If in doubt, two fun-loving dogs will help you on your way.

Try to make time to visit The Falcon in Littleborough, before catching your train maybe. Plentiful and inexpensive food served. Either catch the bus outside The Summit, or walk 2½km along "The Rochdale canal," that is.

Recommended stops: The Summit Inn, the Dog and Partridge (known by some local wags as the Dog and Dagger) because of a bar-room altercation over a game of cards — some time ago, relax.)

Don't forget the INSECT REPELLENT!

Hillsides are dotted with shale heaps – old mining waste. Just keep going roughly SE, picking up the path when you can.

This is moorland walking with a vengeance! Good on the bare, boulder-strewn tops, tough in the moist, marshy and tussocky valleys.

Crook Hill (408m)
Cairn
Turn Slack Hill

The Long Causeway – old pack horse route over to Ramsden.

Path is sometimes unclear. General direction: SE, until Turn Slack Hill, then S. If you can see the wall descending Ringing Pots Hill, then make for that.

Blackstone Edge, White House, Hollingworth Lane, Littleborough.

Fox Stones

Ringing Pots Hill

Cuckoo Hill

Pasture House

Noisy dogs

Lane

Cylinders track

Bench

A6033

down

SUMMIT

PH–The Summit

Ask about walks up to the White House, the resurrection of the Rochdale canal, and the safe that was fished out of the pool in Summit quarry in 1984.

Summit must be one of the friendliest places in the North West! Spend a couple of hours here – it's probably best not to try the climb up to the Pennine Way just yet anyway.

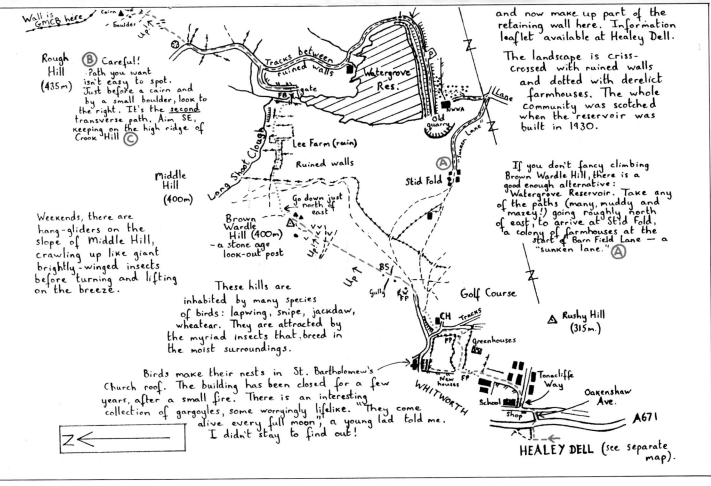

Wall is GMCB here

Cairn
Boulder
up?

Rough Hill (435m)

(B) Careful! Path you want isn't easy to spot. Just before a cairn and by a small boulder, look to the right. It's the second transverse path. Aim SE, keeping on the high ridge of Crook Hill (C)

Middle Hill (400m)

Tracks between ruined walls

FB gate

Watergrove Res.

P

NVWA

Old quarry

Lane

and now make up part of the retaining wall here. Information leaflet available at Healey Dell.

The landscape is criss-crossed with ruined walls and dotted with derelict farmhouses. The whole community was scotched when the reservoir was built in 1930.

Long Shot Clough

Lee Farm (ruin)

Ruined walls

(A)

Stid Fold

"Sunken Lane"

If you don't fancy climbing Brown Wardle Hill, there is a good enough alternative: Watergrove Reservoir. Take any of the paths (many, muddy and mazey!) going roughly north of east, to arrive at Stid Fold, a colony of farmhouses at the start of Barn Field Lane — a "sunken lane." (A)

Weekends, there are hang-gliders on the slope of Middle Hill, crawling up like giant brightly-winged insects before turning and lifting on the breeze.

Go down just north of east

Brown Wardle Hill (400m) — a stone age look-out post

up

up

BS

Gully FP

Golf Course

Rushy Hill (315m.)

These hills are inhabited by many species of birds: lapwing, snipe, jackdaw, wheatear. They are attracted by the myriad insects that breed in the moist surroundings.

CH Tracks

FP

Greenhouses

Birds make their nests in St. Bartholomew's Church roof. The building has been closed for a few years, after a small fire. There is an interesting collection of gargoyles, some worryingly lifelike. "They come alive every full moon", a young lad told me. I didn't stay to find out!

WHITWORTH

New houses

FP

Tonacliffe Way

Oakenshaw Ave.

School

shop

A671

N ←

HEALEY DELL (see separate map).

N ↑

Drain

Green Withens Res.

Blackstone Edge (472m)

Robin Hood's Bed

Withens Moor

The Pennine Way roughly follows the GMCB for 16km, from Blackstone Edge to the A635 on Saddleworth Moor.

Redmires the grim. This is where the rainfall sits on the fence, as if it were, largely undecided as to which side of the watershed to descend. Tackle it on a dry day and the rusty-coloured gauge is bearable. There are makeshift bridges, too.

Aim for the mast on the far side of the M62 valley. They line of cairns guides you too.

Line of cairns guides you too.

Longden End Brook

Redmires

This is the tenth (and thankfully the last) time you cross a motorway on the GMCB. It's also the highest (400m.)

Hoop and cross

M62

M62

Mast

Groundwork (see below) is attacking Redmires, aiming to produce a walkable raft across the slutch. Some purists are up in arms — part of the fun, they say, is the struggle against air, water, earth, and any combination of them. Redmires needs a raft, they say, like a cod needs a vest.

Interestingly, there is much evidence that, a millenium or more ago, there were vast tracts of forest on these now desolate slopes. (withens = willows).

So what was Robin Hood doing up here, of all places? It's a far cry from the merrie dells and glades of Sherwood. Local legend has it that the outlaw was flushed from Littleborough (3 km to the west) to escape to a bolt-hole on the rocky slopes below the Edge. There is no trace of a building here now... or is there? As with the weird arrangement of rocks on Chelburn Moor, viewed from a certain angle, and if your imagination leads that way...

The place-name "Robin Hood" has been a teaser throughout our journey. Remember the Picking Rods above Mellor? The Wells at Helmshore and Healey Dell? There is a village called Robin Hood, 2½ km north of Appley Bridge, named after the mine around which the community grew. And as we drew nearer to our goal in Longdendale, the tales of the outlaw start to proliferate. Either the Robin we know and love was a much-travelled fellow, or there's something else afoot, apart from the weary GMCB-er.

(To be continued).

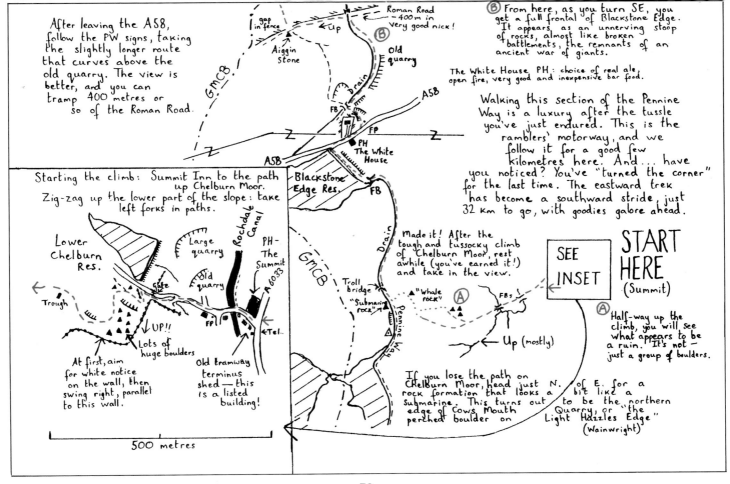

After leaving the A58, follow the PW signs, taking the slightly longer route that curves above the old quarry. The view is better, and you can tramp 400 metres or so of the Roman Road.

Roman Road ~400m in very good nick!

GmCB

gap in fence

Aiggin Stone

Up

B

Old quarry

Drain

FB

A58

FP

PH The White House

A58

Blackstone Edge Res.

FB

Ⓑ From here, as you turn SE, you get a full frontal of Blackstone Edge. It appears as an unnerving stoop of rocks, almost like broken battlements, the remnants of an ancient war of giants.

The White House, PH: choice of real ale, open fire, very good and inexpensive bar food.

Walking this section of the Pennine Way is a luxury after the tussle you've just endured. This is the ramblers' motorway, and we follow it for a good few kilometres here. And... have you noticed? You've "turned the corner" for the last time. The eastward trek has become a southward stride, just 32 km to go, with goodies galore ahead.

Starting the climb: Summit Inn to the path up Chelburn Moor. Zig-zag up the lower part of the slope: take left forks in paths.

Lower Chelburn Res.

Large quarry

Rochdale Canal

Old quarry

PH - The Summit

A6033

Gate

Trough

FP

↓UP!!

←Tel.

Lots of huge boulders

At first, aim for white notice on the wall, then swing right, parallel to this wall.

Old tramway terminus shed — this is a listed building!

GmCB

Drain

Made it! After the tough and tussocky climb of Chelburn Moor, rest awhile (you've earned it!) and take in the view.

Troll bridge

"Submarine rock"

"whale rock"

Ⓐ

Pennine Way

FBs!

SEE INSET

START HERE (Summit)

Ⓐ Half-way up the climb, you will see what appears to be a ruin. It's not — just a group of boulders.

← Up (mostly)

If you lose the path on Chelburn Moor, head just N. of E. for a rock formation that looks a bit like a submarine. This turns out to be the northern edge of Cows Mouth Quarry, or "the Light Hazzles Edge" (Wainwright) perched boulder on

500 metres

The Amnon Wrigley Memorial Stone.

The Dinner Stone.
Looking north-west, towards White Hill.

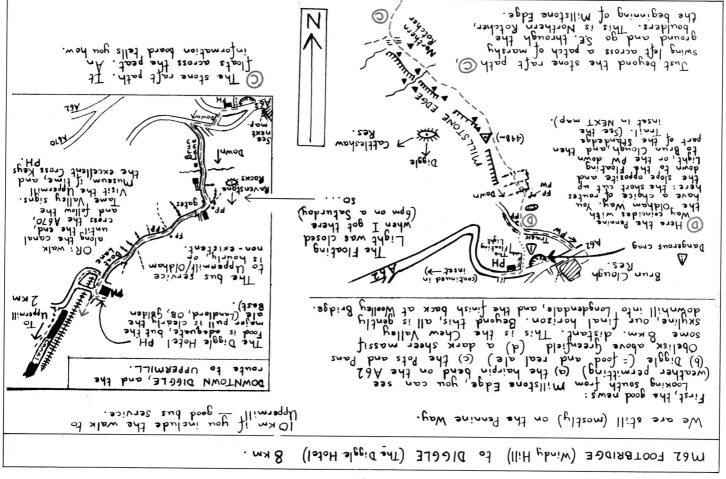

We are re-introduced to the boot-hungry gunge on the way up to the cairn. Not so bad after Redmires, though, and there are more of those "horizontal fence" bridges.

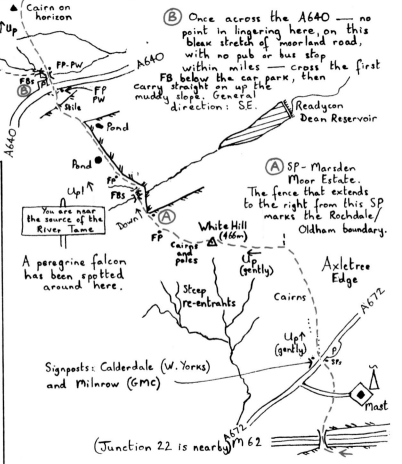

ON ROCKS AND A POET OF THE EDGES

"Where the old rock stands
                weathered and lone
And black as night, turned into stone,
There's a green church I call my own."

Ammon Wrigley – "The Dinner Stone". *

The poet's ashes were scattered, at his wish, by the Dinner Stone on Sept. 14th, 1946. Between the unmistakable black overhang of the Stone and the Trig. Point, there is something of a Wrigley family plot. The Memorial Plaques Rock offers shelter from an easterly, as well as fine views over the valley below.

The poems are worth a read, too.

It's a good place to linger awhile, to re-gather your courage and tranquillity.

* Taken from "With Ammon Wrigley in Saddleworth" by Sam Seville.
(Saddleworth Historical Society 1984).

Cross-section of a DRY-STONE WALL

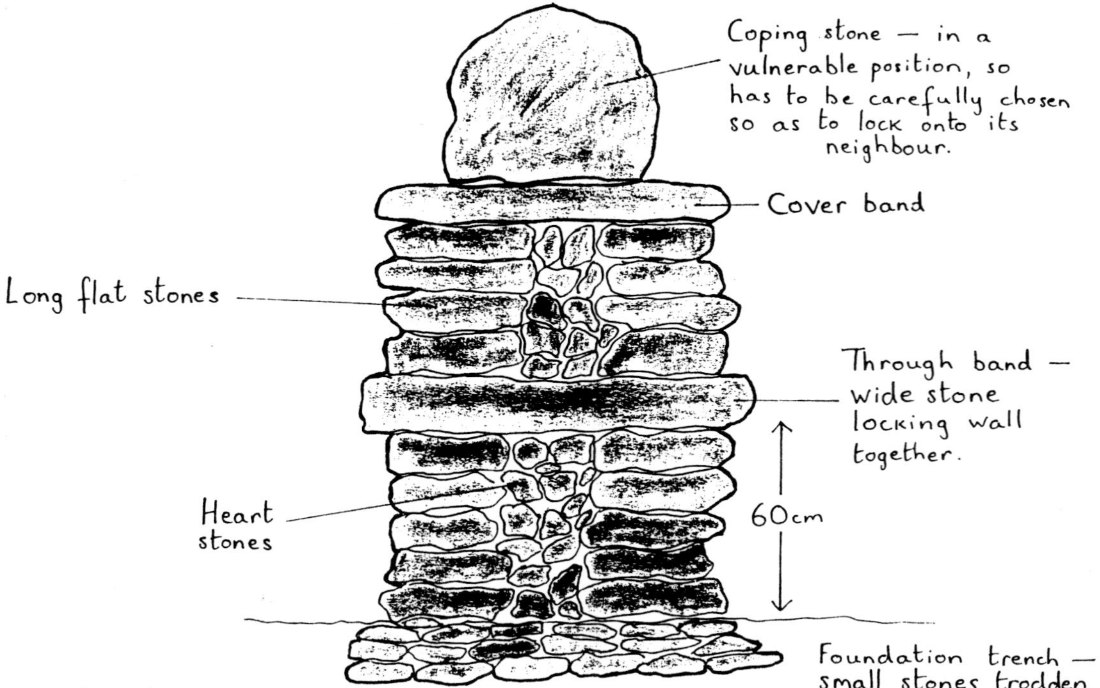

Coping stone — in a vulnerable position, so has to be carefully chosen so as to lock onto its neighbour.

Cover band

Long flat stones

Through band — wide stone locking wall together.

Heart stones

60cm

Foundation trench — small stones trodden in to depth of 15cm.

This page is based on the article "Dry Stone Walls" by Peter Chantree which appeared in "The Rambler", Dec 1988

The War Memorial by the "Pots and Pans" stone.

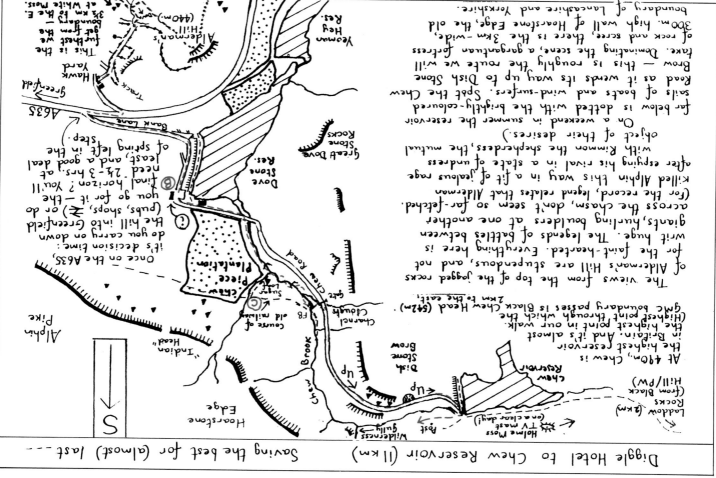

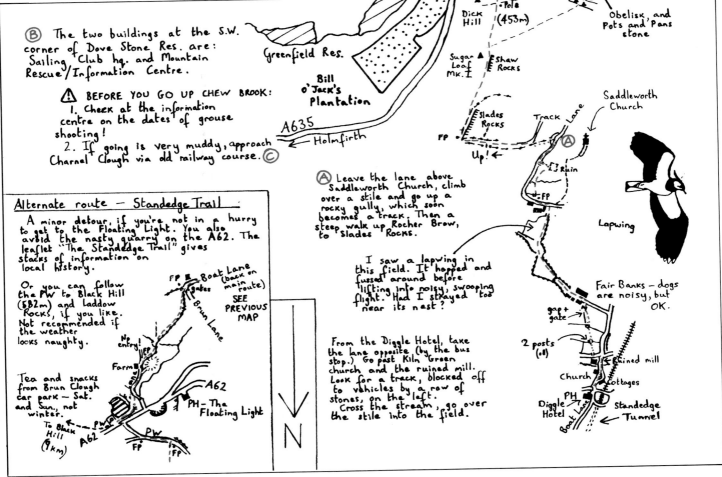

Ⓑ The two buildings at the S.W. corner of Dove Stone Res. are: Sailing Club hq. and Mountain Rescue/Information Centre.

⚠ BEFORE YOU GO UP CHEW BROOK:
1. Check at the information centre on the dates of grouse shooting!
2. If going is very muddy, approach Charnel Clough via old railway course. Ⓒ

Greenfield Res.

Bill o'Jack's Plantation

A635
← Holmfirth

Dick Hill
Pole (453m)

Obelisk, and Pots and Pans stone

Sugar Loaf Mk. I ▲
Shaw Rocks

Slades Rocks
Track Lane
Saddleworth Church

FP
Up! ←

Ruin
FP

Ⓐ Leave the lane above Saddleworth Church, climb over a stile and go up a rocky gully, which soon becomes a track. Then a steep walk up Rocher Brow, to Slades Rocks.

I saw a lapwing in this field. It hopped and fussed around before lifting into noisy, swooping flight. Had I strayed too near its nest?

Lapwing

From the Diggle Hotel, take the lane opposite (by the bus stop.) Go past Kiln Green church and the ruined mill. Look for a track, blocked off to vehicles by a row of stones, on the left. Cross the stream, go over the stile into the field.

Fair Banks — dogs are noisy, but OK.

gap + gate
2 posts (off)
ruined mill
Church
Cottages
PH
Diggle Hotel
Boat Lane
Standedge Tunnel

Alternate route — Standedge Trail

A minor detour, if you're not in a hurry to get to the Floating Light. You also avoid the nasty quarry on the A62. The leaflet "The Standedge Trail" gives stacks of information on local history.

Or you can follow the PW to Black Hill (582m) and Laddow Rocks, if you like. Not recommended if the weather looks naughty.

Tea and snacks from Brun Clough car park — Sat. and Sun., not winter.

FP
Boat Lane (back on main route)
gates
Brun Lane
SEE PREVIOUS MAP
No entry!
Farm

A62
PH — The Floating Light

To Black Hill (9km)
A62
PW
FP
FP

↓ N

Chew Reservoir to Woolley Bridge (7 km)

INSECT REPELLENT!

A Lord of Misrule.

If you want something to ponder on as you tackle the long and easy descent into Longdendale, you may like to consider once more the many Robin Hood place-names. They are scattered across the north country, mostly in sparsely-populated areas. On the GMCB we have encountered the Picking Rods, two Wells, a village called Robin Hood, and the Bed below Blackstone Edge. Add to these Robin Hood's Stone, flung from Werneth Low, 6 km to the west, on the old Lancashire/Cheshire border.

So who was the real Robin Hood? Once we start digging, as it were, we find that the ground shifts beneath us. For the better-known sanitised version (outlaw, forest-dweller, robber of the idle rich, champion of the lowly and the free) has its origins, it seems, deep in the pagan past. The Old Religion — Celtic, pre-Christian, the roots of latter-day witchcraft — was (still is?) most resilient away from the towns, out here on the boundary.

Robert Graves discovered that the male leader of a coven was often called Robin. Links have been explored with Robin Goodfellow, Puck, Pan, the Green Man, and most interestingly of all, Cernunnos, the ancient Celtic god of the hunt, and Lord of the Underworld. He was depicted as the horned god of the forests, sometimes appearing in disguise ... with a hood over his head.

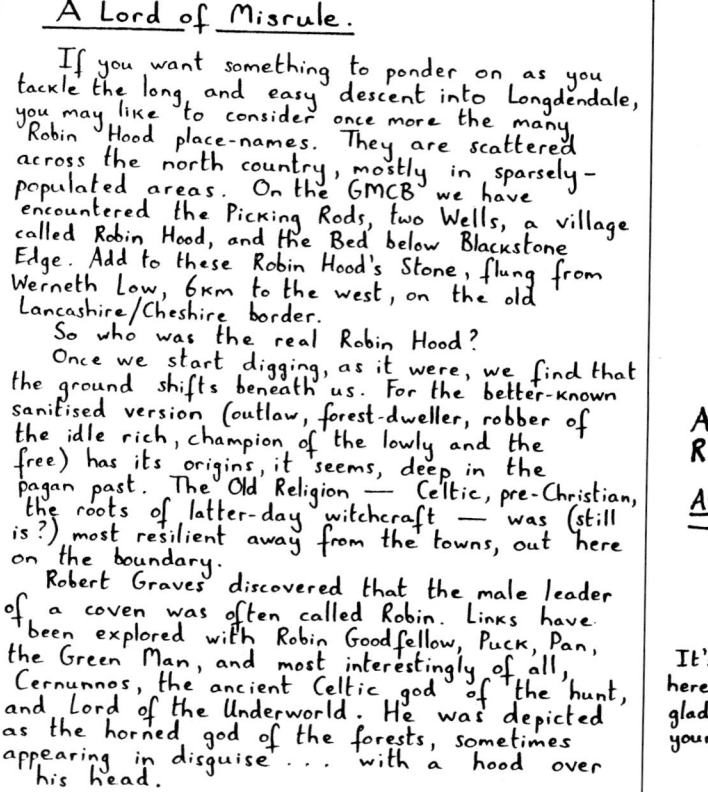

For more detail, see 1:5000 map on next page.

Woolley Bridge

(This is where we came in)

Hollingworth

Arnfield Reservoir
A628

Meadowbank Farm

Green Lane

E Go through the gap in the hedgerow (you will see Meadowbank Farm ahead, on your right) Look left, and locate the gap in the wall. This will bring you out onto the rural end of Green Lane.

You may see pheasants in these woods.

D Don't get too excited by the name; it's just a prosaic and functional wooden affair, of Dutch origin, for some reason. Cross the small stream and follow the path up into the woods.

It's round about here that you'll be glad you brought your insect repellent.

Ladder stile

Stile

Field

Stile

D Devil's Bridge

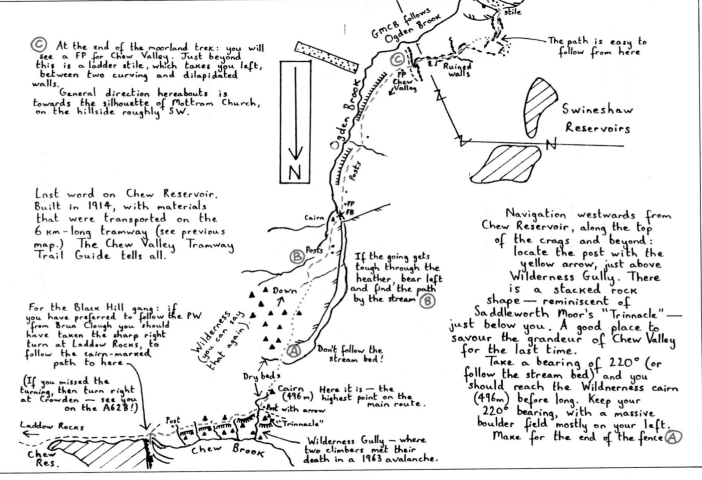

C At the end of the moorland trek: you will see a FP for Chew Valley. Just beyond this is a ladder stile, which takes you left, between two curving and dilapidated walls.

General direction hereabouts is towards the silhouette of Mottram Church, on the hillside roughly SW.

GmCB follows Ogden Brook

stile

The path is easy to follow from here

C
FP Chew Valley

Ruined walls

Swineshaw Reservoirs

N

Ogden Brook

Posts

Last word on Chew Reservoir. Built in 1914, with materials that were transported on the 6 km-long tramway (see previous map.) The Chew Valley Tramway Trail Guide tells all.

FP FB

Cairn

B Posts

If the going gets tough through the heather, bear left and find the path by the stream **B**

Down

For the Black Hill gang: if you have preferred to follow the PW from Brun Clough you should have taken the sharp right turn at Laddow Rocks, to follow the cairn-marked path to here

Wilderness (you can say that again)

A Don't follow the stream bed!

(If you missed the turning, then turn right at Crowden — see you on the A628!)

Dry beds

Laddow Rocks

Chew Res.

Post

Cairn (496m) Here it is — the highest point on the main route.

Post with arrow "Trinnacle"

Chew Brook

Wilderness Gully — where two climbers met their death in a 1963 avalanche.

Navigation westwards from Chew Reservoir, along the top of the crags and beyond: locate the post with the yellow arrow, just above Wilderness Gully. There is a stacked rock shape — reminiscent of Saddleworth Moor's "Trinnacle" — just below you. A good place to savour the grandeur of Chew Valley for the last time.

Take a bearing of 220° (or follow the stream bed) and you should reach the Wilderness cairn (496m) before long. Keep your 220° bearing, with a massive boulder field mostly on your left. Make for the end of the fence **A**

As a bonus, and as it would be a pity to lose your way at this stage, here is the last kilometre or so in glorious 1:5000.

250 metres

The End!

To Glossop

Dinting 2 km

Shop

PH

PH

Woolley Close

A57

Taylor St.

The Boulevard

Holly Grove Lodge

L

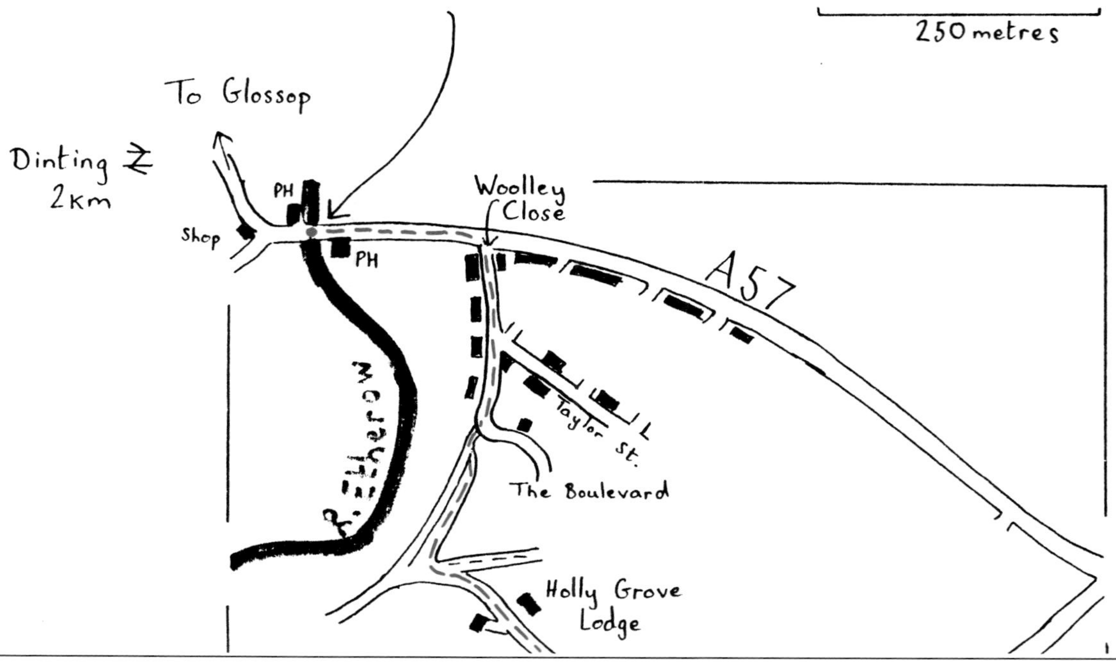

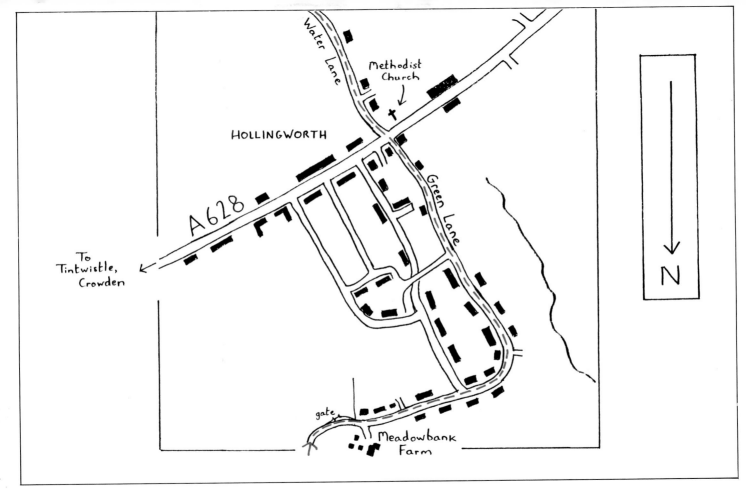

HOLLINGWORTH

Water Lane

Methodist Church

A628

To Tintwistle, Crowden

Green Lane

gate

Meadowbank Farm

N

THE END?

So how do you feel as you stand on Woolley Bridge, the Etherow running below you and the traffic on the A57 lumbering by?

What have you achieved? You are possibly fitter and more erudite than the last time you stood here. You have many memories of the round - perhaps you want to mull over them as you sink a pint in the Woolley Bridge (Bass, Stones) or the Spread Eagle (Murphy's, rock and roll on a Saturday night). Reminiscences of the people that you've met, the widely varied scenery that you've trekked through, the glimpses of History, some so ancient that they merged into Legend, that you've been granted, the pints you've supped, the plants and animals you've spotted: all these memories you may turn over in your mind at leisure in the months and years to come.

You may feel, as I did, a sense of anti-climax. It was about five minutes later in the lounge of the Woolley Bridge that the question surfaced: What next?

Perhaps the Offa's Dyke, or the Coast-to-Coast, or even the Pennine Way in it's entirety. Or how about discovering another Boundary Walk - Derbyshire sprang to mind. Varied scenery, fabulous walking country, and enough towns for pit-stops along the way. Or how about the Greater London Boundary?

Oh yes - the bug had bitten all right.

And now, as we part company, I hope that for you too this is just the beginning. I hope that you too have come to appreciate the marvellous head-clearing qualities of putting one foot in front of the other across high ground or on peripheral paths, as you make your careful, steadfast way into the unknown.

Graham Phythian 1988-91

APPENDIX

Some useful telephone numbers

(1) Travel

Bus enquiries   061 228 7811

British Rail   061 832 8353

(2) Accommodation - Some B + B close to the route
Additional information from the relevant tourist
centre - see below
Distance from the main GMCB route given in
brackets.

Needhams Farm, Uplands Rd, Werneth Low
Gee Cross   061 368 4610   (6km)

The Royal Oak, Sheffield Rd, Glossop
                   045 74 64054   (2km)

Royal Oak Hotel, Buxton Rd, Disley
                   0663 62380   (1km)

King William, Manchester Rd, Wilmslow   (0km)

Spinney Hotel (Poynton Station)
                   0625 871397   (0km)

Tatton Dale Farm, Ashley Rd, Knutsford
                   0565 - 54692   (1km)

Church Green Hotel, Higher Lane, Lymm
(near Lymm Dam)   09259 - 2068   (2km)

For the Glazebrook - Blackrod section, it is suggested
that you use Wigan as a central point of departure.

Black Bull, 101 High St, Belmont
                   0204 - 81370   (1km)

Loe Farm, Redisher Lane, Hawkshaw, Bury
                   0204 883668   (½km)

Gaghills House Hotel, Waterfoot, Rossendale
                   0706 - 830359   (4km)

The Sun Hotel, Featherstall Rd, Littleborough
                   0706 78957   (3km)

The Shepherd's Boy, Manchester Rd, Standedge
                   0484 - 844778   (1½km)

93

(3) INFORMATION CENTRES

Manchester Town Hall	061 236 2035
Glossop	045 74 5920
Lyme Hall	0663 62023
Stockport	061 480 0315
Quarry Bank Mill, Styal	0625 527468
Altrincham	061 941 7337
Tatton Park	0565 54822
Dunham Massey	061 941 1025
Trafford	061 872 2101
Wigan	0942 825677
Three Sisters	0942 720453
Pennington Flash	0942 605253
Bolton	0204 22311
Great House Barn (Lever Park)	0204 691549
Jumbles	0204 853360
East Lancs Steam Railway	061 764 7790
Rossendale	0706 217777
Healey Dell	0706 350459
Rochdale	0706 356592
Littleborough Coach House	0706 78481
Holmfirth (for Saddleworth)	0484 684992